W9-CSR-077

CLASSIC

CALENDARS

CLASSIC Coca-Cola

CALENDARS

BY ALLAN PETRETTI
& CHRIS H. BEYER

ANTIQUE TRADER BOOKS

A Division of Krause Publications

Iola, Wisconsin

DEDICATION

The authors extend their sincere thanks to the following for their important contributions to this book: The Coca-Cola Company, of Atlanta Georgia; Phillip F. Mooney, Archives Manager of the Coca-Cola Company; Sharon and Joe Happle; Gordon Breslow; Vincent and Ann Jacono; Larry, Beth, and Josh Markowitz; Bob Newman; and "The Barefoot Boy," Danny MacGrant.

ISBN: 1-58221-002-0

Library of Congress Catalog Card Number: 99-61634

Editor: Allan W. Miller
Assistant Editor: Wendy Chia-Klesch
Designer: Heather Ealey

Manufactured in the United States of America

Published by
Antique Trader Books
A Division of Krause Publications

To order additional copies of this book, or to obtain a free catalog, please call 800-258-0929.
For information about our book publishing program, please call: 715-445-2214.

Krause Publications
700 E. State Street
Iola, WI 54990-0001

CONTENTS

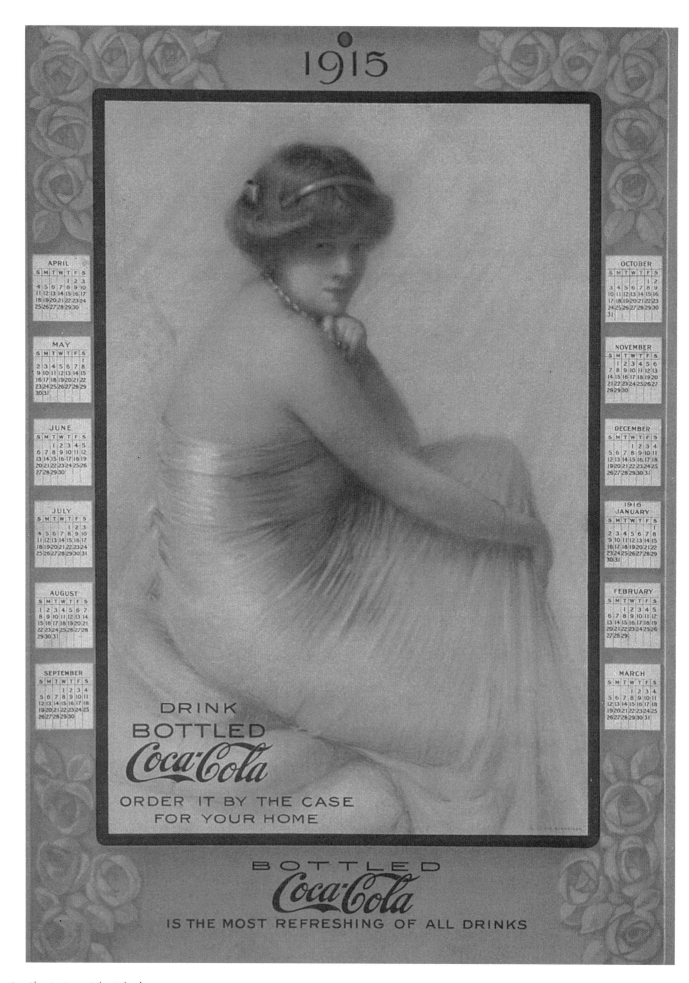

COCA-COLA® TODAY RANKS AS THE MOST RECOGNIZED TRADEMARK
IN THE WORLD. YET, AS WITH MOST GREAT ENTERPRISES, THIS POPULAR
BRAND HAD HUMBLE BEGINNINGS.

The history of the soft drink we now know as Coca-Cola began with a formula known as "French Wine of Coca," developed by John Styth Pemberton in the mid-1880s. Shortly after it was first offered as a soft drink, the name was changed to Coca-Cola. In failing health at the time, Pemberton sold a percentage of his financial ownership of the beverage to other investors even before it had reached the first bloom of its unforeseen potential. In 1888, Asa G. Candler, a prominent Atlanta pharmacist, bought out the remaining interest owned by Pemberton, along with that which had been purchased by the initial group of investors, for a grand total of $2,300.

A few years later, with the founding of The Coca-Cola Company in 1892, the world's greatest marketing machine was off and running. Few companies in existence—then or now—have achieved and maintained the positive image that comes to mind when one thinks of the Coca-Cola trademark. In large part, this tremendous success and acceptance stems from Coca-Cola's use of pleasant, uplifting images that, for more than a century, have been used to promote a very simple product. Those images have appeared on hundreds of items which are continuously infused into everyday life.

With the emergence of high-speed printing technology in the 1880s, a new medium that manufacturing and businesses could effectively use to promote their products was born. Prior to that time, point of sale advertising was primarily limited to the use of hand-painted signs. Since these signs were labor intensive to produce, they were not a major factor in American commerce. Quick to sense the potential of colorful, mass-produced advertising signage, The Coca-Cola Company began making use of commercial printing techniques and technology to promote its products.

Prior to the founding of The Coca-Cola Company, a small printed cardboard sign had been used to promote the aforementioned "French Wine of Coca." In 1886, the first known printed piece to be purchased for distribution and promotion of the Coca-Cola soft drink took the form of an advertising ticket bearing a printed "parody" and the name "Coca-Cola." Later, in 1890, printed posters, some small tin signs, and Coca-Cola books were issued as advertising. Then, in 1891, a colorful calendar, with tear-off pages for each month of the year, was printed and distributed. Within a few short years, The Coca-Cola Company began the regular and continuous use of calendars as an advertising medium.

Coca-Cola calendars, with their wonderful and compelling images of attractive people (particularly pretty young women), provide a visual chronicle of changes that have occurred in fashion and society as times have changed. Although the concept of using a calendar to advertise a

John Styth Pemberton, creator of the drink that would later be called Coca-Cola.

product seems rather basic today, one must consider that the first mass-produced advertising calendars did not appear on the scene until the mid-1880s. Until that time, the technology to produce hundreds or thousands of high-quality multicolor images on paper simply did not exist.

Before the emergence of radio and television in the twentieth century, the most common way to expose the consuming public to an advertising message had been via the newspaper. But the advertising novelty trade, which had its birth in Ohio in the mid-1880s, caught on like wildfire with American industry. What better way to reach an audience with a promotional message than to provide businesses—soda fountains, in the case of our area of interest—with a useful calendar that provided the functional purpose of giving the day of the month, while also extolling the virtues of a glass of "Delicious" and "Refreshing" Coca-Cola.

The story of The Coca-Cola Company's involvement with calendars is lengthy, dynamic, and interesting. Starting with its first advertising calendar in 1891, we now can count—and continue to enjoy—more than one hundred years of extraordinary examples of this timeless promotional medium. Today, the scarce remaining examples of these early treasures have become valued pieces in collections of advertising art memorabilia. Coca-Cola advertising calendars have proven to be even more prodigious in use and longevity than the renowned advertising serving tray, which saw its functional production end in the 1960s.

In addition to the annual issuance of a standard calendar by The Coca-Cola Company, beginning in 1897 many individual bottlers also had calendars produced for their local markets. Some of these are exceedingly rare, and their art is highly desirable. Due to the sheer number of calendars produced both over the years and within a given year, there is ample subject matter for undertaking a serious examination of Coca-Cola calendar art.

The most important and strategic use of advertising calendars by The Coca-Cola Company occurred from 1890-1940, when soda fountains, drug stores, and other retail outlets provided a perfect setting for the calendar to be displayed as an advertising medium. The Company continued to issue calendars well into the second half of the twentieth century, but the role of the calendar in the advertising program was eventually eclipsed by television, radio, and other print media. As a result, our focus here will be on the first five decades of Coca-Cola calendars—the fifty-year period when the calendars themselves were a most significant part of The Company's advertising program, and the period of primary collecting interest to today's collector.

This reference book, the second in a planned series following publication of the *Classic Coca-Cola Serving Trays* volume in 1998, is intended for a wide and diverse audience. First, it is for anyone interested in the marvelous art displayed on Coca-Cola calendars. Second, individuals who are fascinated by the captivating history of The Coca-Cola Company will enjoy reading about these attractive products and their long history, as well. Finally, persons who want to learn more about the development of print advertising materials in America will find the subject matter lively and informative. As was done in the book on serving trays, other Coca-Cola advertising collateral will also be pictured and described. Collectors will also be provided with grading and collecting guidelines for the always-popular calendars. Individuals wishing to acquire such pieces will find this information invaluable as an in-depth, comprehensive reference that provides infinitely more detail than what can be found in a general price guide.

Over the years, Coca-Cola calendars have provided many alluring and colorful images. In addition to featuring the pictorial theme of lovely young ladies, we find bi-planes, tennis and golf scenes, and the wonderful art of famous illustrators such as Norman Rockwell and N. C. Wyeth. The colorful commemoration of the 50th anniversary of The Coca-Cola Company, along with other interesting and diverse subjects, were also reflected on calendar issues over the decades. Because of the beauty and appeal of these pieces, it is no wonder that some consider them to be the highest art form of Coca-Cola advertising memorabilia. As such, the authors of this book are happy to share this colorful anthology with you.

The Coca-Cola Company used a number of types of calendars over the years. To make identifying these different types of calendars easier, we have described below the nine most widely used types and have identified them as A through I. Rather than repeatedly describe each calendar's characteristics, letter types found in each calendar's description will correspond to these drawings.

A. Stock Art—Standard piece of art produced so advertising can be imprinted.

B. Embossed Cardstock—Grommet hole at top, with a calendar pad stapled on.

C. Embossed Cardstock—Grommet hole at top, with calendar months actually printed on the image.

D. Cardstock Print—Grommet hole at top; full-size calendar pad stapled at bottom.

E. Cardstock Print—Drilled hole at top; smaller size calendar pad stapled to print.

F. Paper Print—Metal strip at top with hanger; stapled pad at bottom.

G. Paper Print—Multi-page calendar (two months on each page for a total of six prints); cardboard or metal strip at top, with hanger.

H. Paper Print—Multi-page calendar (two months on each page for a total of six prints); fold-over center stapled; hole drilled at top.

I. Paper Print—Multi-page calendar; small home calendars; hole drilled at top.

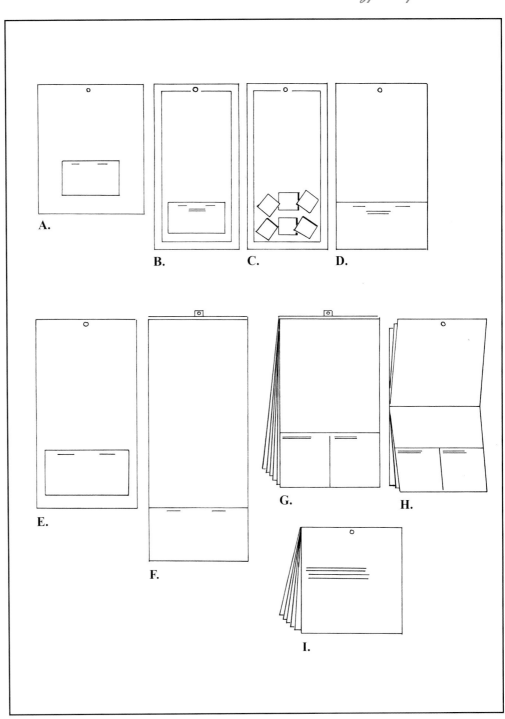

A.

B.   C.   D.

E.

F.

G.   H.

I.

THE DEVELOPMENT OF EARLY PRINTING
AND ADVERTISING SPECIALTY TRADES IN AMERICA

Chapter 1

The years preceding the founding of The Coca-Cola Company were a watershed for technological development. Europe and America were experiencing an explosion of new information, leading to better ways of doing things both faster and more efficiently. In the forty years from 1860-1900, the world was transformed with breakthroughs in transportation, medicine, and communication. In 1876, Alexander Graham Bell invented the telephone, and just one year later, Thomas A. Edison invented the phonograph. In 1880, Edison and J. W Swan independently devised the use of electric lights. That same year, the first street lights appeared in New York City.

During this period, events were occurring that would set the stage for the birth of The Coca-Cola Company. In the 1870s, the concept of the "soda fountain" was in its infancy. Colored and flavored non-alcoholic soda waters were being produced to quench the thirst of a society that was experiencing a multitude of new leisure products. After the 1876 Centennial celebration commemorating the 100th anniversary of the nation's founding, new businesses emerged which were designed to provide comfortable surroundings for people to congregate and exchange pleasantries, while enjoying refreshing soft drinks. Ultimately, these became the ever-popular soda fountain—a true icon of the American lifestyle.

With growing cities and an explosion in rail travel, America of the 1880s and 1890s was quickly transforming into a mobile society. New industrial firms employed thousands of employees who were, in turn, becoming avid consumers. A further signal of things to come was Karl Benz's development of a single-cylinder engine for a motor car. Important new developments related to printing were also occurring. Before examining how the first calendars were printed, and discussing just why they were chosen as an advertising medium, a brief history of the evolution of image transfer technology is in order.

EARLY PRINTING PROCESS DEVELOPMENT

The earliest productive process of printing an image onto metal was known as chromo-lithography, an outgrowth of the process of lithography that had been discovered by Aloys Senefelder, a German printer, in the 1790s. Since the chromo-lithography process involved the use of limestone plates to transfer images, it is also known as "stone lithography." In the most basic terms, the process itself is based on the premise that oil and water don't mix. First, an artist, using lithographic crayons containing an oil-based ink, would draw images and colors onto a limestone plate. Once the images were completed, water would be applied to the entire surface. Printing ink, which would naturally adhere to the image area (as defined by the artist's lithographic crayons) but not to the remainder of the plate, was then applied. Paper could then be placed directly onto the plate, allowing the inked image areas alone to transfer onto the paper, thus creating a printed impression.

This process was employed for printing on paper long before metals were used as the surface to be imprinted. Some refinement of the technique would have to be found before it could be applied to high-quality printing on metal—a somewhat more complex task due to the relative inflexibility of metal, and the difficulty in keeping a metal surface perfectly flat and smooth during the printing process. When the image on an inked limestone plate was applied to a metal surface, for example, some irregularities in ink coverage usually occurred, resulting in less-than-crisp images. The first printed metal advertising signs produced in the early 1890s were not of high quality due to this problem. But an answer to this vexing situation was soon to be discovered.

The Meek Company in Ohio, in the mid-1890s, worked with another local firm to develop a highly effective method of printing onto metal—an adaptation of the process now known as offset-lithography. It was discovered that crisp images could be achieved by using a rubber sheet, or blanket, to serve as an intermediate surface to accept the inked image of the printing plate, and subsequently transfer this ink to the surface of the metal. In other words, direct contact between the printing plate and the surface to be printed was avoided. Perhaps best of all, rubber also exhibited the flexibility to be compatible with both limestone and metal surfaces. As a result, this new process allowed for the high-quality and strikingly vibrant metal lithography so often seen in the early years of the twentieth century.

A decided drawback of the early chromo-lithography process, at least as far as the mass production of printed items was concerned, was that it required that a new plate be prepared for each primary color and shade of color. This being the case, many of the more complex pictures to be reproduced required as many as twenty separate runs through the press! Nevertheless, the finished products resulting from this type of printing are truly works of art. The color definition and saturation provided by separate runs for each subtle shade made these pieces absolutely stunning in their vivid portrayal of images. Many consider these early treasures highly superior to those produced after stone lithography was eventually replaced by photo-lithography—the latter process being adapted because it proved more cost-effective and more productive.

PHOTO-LITHOGRAPHY

Around 1900, the techniques for a much more efficient and productive printing process were discovered. This process utilized photography to provide the color separations for printing plates. The process involved only four color plates—one each in cyan, magenta, yellow, and black. An etched-dot pattern, created photographically, was formed on each printing plate. With this method, tones and shades of the pattern could be differentiated and incorporated to produce images in the full spectrum of actual colors. And, most importantly, all of this could be accomplished in only four press runs. This process proved to be inherently faster and cheaper than chromo-lithography. Faster drying times and fewer press runs resulted in a diminished opportunity for errors and the more cost-effective use of available labor. The process progressed even further in later years, when superior zinc plates replaced those made of limestone.

The improved productivity provided by photo-lithography, combined with new presses capable of running as much as seven times faster than the old flatbed presses, relegated chromo-lithography to the status of a dying art, and most printers of advertising signs, calendars, and serving trays began converting to photo-lithography in the second decade of the twentieth century.

The trained eye can easily distinguish a calendar printed with the chromo-lithography process as opposed one printed using photo-lithography. Early stone-litho printed pieces, including those produced for Coca-Cola through 1914, exhibit large color separation dots and the incomparable deep multi-colors that result from separate color runs for each individual shade. Most of the later photo-lithography items exhibit a fine dot screen, which results from using the four-color photographic color separations. The depth of color of the original stone-litho printing is marvelous. Consequently, the calendars, trays, and other pictorial advertising pieces that were produced by use of the stone-litho process are truly regarded as works of art.

THE FIRST YEARS OF THE ADVERTISING SPECIALTY TRADE

The development and enhancement of printing processes was a springboard for a new industry in the United States. "Specialty advertising" as a trade was an idea first conceived by a printer named William Shaw, who operated a business based in Coshocton, Ohio. By the mid-1880s, Shaw had developed a successful business printing small advertising trade cards. These colorful cards used attractive, interesting, and sometimes humorous graphics to promote a variety of products. Indeed, trade cards were the earliest kind of mass-produced, colorfully printed advertising items.

At about the same time, two competing Coshocton newspapermen also sensed the potential for "novelty" advertising items. J. F. Meek and H. D. Beach expanded their own newspaper businesses to include specialty advertising printing. In 1887, Meek developed the idea of printing colorful advertisements on school bags. With instant success at hand, Meek followed up with a variety of other mass-use items as advertising subjects. Some of these item included backs of chairs, thermometers, newspaper bags, grocery aprons, fans, and calendars. Meek's new company was named The Tuscarora Advertising Company.

In 1888, H. D. Beach, also of Coshocton, entered the advertising specialty business with a firm known as The Standard Advertising Company. From the start, the largest share of this company's business involved the production of advertising calendars. With business increasing dramatically, the printing firms soon added sales representatives to their staff, and these individuals were charged with promoting advertising items throughout the entire country. These two companies—Tuscarora Advertising and Standard Advertising—played a pivotal role in leading the way for American businesses to utilize a wide variety of everyday items to display and merchandise their products.

Two of the first firms electing to mass-distribute advertising calendars were the Winchester Firearms Company and Hoods Sarsaparilla. A Winchester Firearms calendar displaying a hunting scene is known to exist for the year 1884. By the late 1880s, many other firms were also using calendars to promote a wide variety of products. Soon, the yet-to-be-formed Coca-Cola Company would follow suit, employing eye-catching advertising calendars to promote its soft drink.

THE ROLE OF ADVERTISING CALENDARS
AND OTHER PROMOTIONAL MATERIALS
IN THE EARLY YEARS OF THE COCA-COLA COMPANY

The genius of Asa G. Candler was demonstrated early in the history of the promotion of Coca-Cola. The *Atlanta Journal* of May 1, 1889, recorded the following prophetic statement: "It has been seen that Asa G. Candler, by the fall of 1888, controlled Coca-Cola. He was the first man in this position who combined the attributes of vision, capital, and energy, which were necessary to the creation of a 'National Beverage'."

Candler's early promotion of his Coca-Cola soft drink quickly grew well beyond the bounds of the Atlanta, Georgia, area. Soda fountains in locations as distant as Norfolk, Virginia, were also offering the new soft drink. An early writer said of Coca-Cola: "It is a new and popular soda fountain drink containing the tonic properties of the wonderful coca plant and the famous cola nuts. It is delicious, refreshing, exhilarating and invigorating and can be found on draught at all popular soda fountains at five cents per glass, and is sold at twenty five cents per bottle by druggists and grocers."

Sales of Coca-Cola increased from 2,171 gallons in 1889 to 8,855 gallons in 1890. But, Candler's highly successful pharmacy in Atlanta was keeping him from devoting all of his energies to the market development of the Coca-Cola soft drink. As a result, he determined that the potential for Coca-Cola was so tremendous that he needed to devote all his efforts to it.

There were some initial uses of advertising collateral in the form of oil cloth signage, an early tin sign, a poster, and newspaper advertising attributed to the year 1890. More importantly, however, the Coca-Cola Company's own *Black Book: History of Coca-Cola* cites that the primary method of promoting the soft drink from the firm's inception was the use of complimentary drink tickets.

Asa Candler's personal recollection was as follows:

"One of the first and most effective methods of advertising Coca-Cola was the distribution and redemption of complimentary tickets entitling the holder to one glass of Coca-Cola free at the soda fountain of some specific dispenser, or in some cases any dispenser of Coca-Cola. An inducement to buy, a dispenser (soda fountain) was promised a distribution of say one hundred free tickets for his benefit. The salesman usually obtained from the dispenser a list and addresses of one hundred of his regular customers to whom the tickets, with a circular letter, were mailed, so timed to reach the potential consumer at about the time this Coca-Cola order was delivered by freight by the dispenser and ready for serving. In filling such order, a liberal supply of point-of-purchase attractive advertising material was packed into a box and accompanied by the shipment of the Coca-Cola. It was my duty to receive the customers' mailing lists, set up with rubber type in a small hand printing press the name of the dealer, and print this name on the specified number of tickets. Young ladies who wrote a neat hand, addressed the envelopes to the persons named on the customers' mailing list: Complimentary tickets were enclosed bearing the dispensers' name (good only at his soda fountain), together with a circular letter, and the letter was sealed and mailed to them. In due season, the dispenser mailed us the tickets for which he exchanged drinks of Coca-Cola. These were checked up and remittance mailed to the customer at five cents each for the tickets. All, or practically all the sales were made through jobbers (salesmen)."

Chapter 2

Asa Griggs Candler, founder of the Coca-Cola Company, made Coca-Cola a national beverage.

What is perhaps most interesting is that the process Candler described in this statement amounted to an early, and very sophisticated, direct mail and fulfillment process. In retrospect, its brilliance was remarkable. Not content to simply sell the Coca-Cola syrup to the fountain service owner, Candler's procedure assured that the product would be sampled by the customer, thereby creating demand. The business or fountain service owner was guaranteed reimbursement for each for the redeemed free drink tickets by the Coca-Cola Company.

In 1891, the first known advertising calendar for Coca-Cola referred to the new drink as "A delightful summer or winter drink. For headache or tired feeling. Relieves mental and physical exhaustion." The calendar listed the business name as Asa G. Candler & Co.—Atlanta, Georgia. There was also a second similar calendar issued in 1891. Hearkening back to its beginnings in a pharmacy, Coca-Cola was marketed in its first years as a refreshing drink with medicinal properties. The earliest promotion slogans were "The ideal Brain Tonic, specific for headache," while others used one word descriptions such as "invigorating" and "exhilarating."

The two calendars issued in 1891 were undoubtedly the first issued by Asa Candler for the promotion of Coca-Cola, given the embryonic stage of The Company. Both were 6-1/2" x 9" in size, and featured attractive young girls. Since The Coca-Cola Company had not yet been incorporated, these calendars bore the name of Asa G. Candler on them. Both featured a pictorial theme that has remained a constant with Coca-Cola over the years: the use of attractive young ladies to promote the beverage. They also used identical ad copy which states: "A delightful Summer or Winter Drink for Headache or Tired Feeling. Relieves Mental or Physical Exhaustion."

It is amazing that examples of these early calendars exist today, and that they have survived the ravages of time in remarkable condition. Highly subject to light, heat, and moisture deterioration, the existence of any paper advertising from more than one hundred years ago is unusual. It is doubtful that more than a few hundred of these calendars were produced, which adds to the rarity of these earliest calendars.

Historical advertising, such as the 1891 Coca-Cola calendars, are highly sought after by collectors. They tell a story about a bygone era when styles and values were very different than they are today. As with other antiques, when viewing them, one can step back to a time before the modern conveniences that we so often take for granted today even existed. It is striking to realize that the 1891 calendar predated the Spanish American war, Theodore Roosevelt's presidency, and the first use of automobiles in the United States. At that time, Los Angeles was little more than a stage stop and minor agricultural trading center in Southern California.

The year 1892 brought about the next major step in the development of the world's most celebrated soft drink. Asa Candler incorporated The Coca-Cola Company as a Georgia Corporation, with authorized capital stock of $100,000. The Company also initiated its first advertising budget in the amount of $11,401, and produced calendars for a second year. This calendar was issued early in the year 1892 and, as such, still carried the name of Asa G. Candler on it rather than The Coca-Cola Company. Unlike the 1891 calendars, the 1892 calendar was designed as a single piece, with small printed pages for each month of the year, and a dominant central picture of a young woman.

An interesting fact about the 1892 calendar is that, until the last decade, this issue was thought by Coca-Cola historians to be the first Coca-Cola advertising calendar. *The Red Barrel*, a publication provided by The Coca-Cola Company to its fountain service customers, stated in a 1928 issue that the 1892 calendar was the first used to promote Coca-Cola. Of course, today we know that two versions of an 1891 calendar were issued, and preceded it.

The World Exposition held in Chicago in 1893 was a showcase of new products and technological development. The Coca-Cola Company was there to promote its soft drink. Visited by people from all over the United States and from around the world, the Exposition provided a marvelous opportunity for broader exposure of the soft drink, and Coca-Cola was a major hit. At this time, many other changes were occurring in America. That same year, Henry Ford built his first car, and Cole Porter, the immortal song writer, was born. It was truly an age of growth and change!

The Coca-Cola Company used its first fountain service backbar sign at the Exposition in 1893. Also making a first appearance were trademarked glass holders made of German nickel silver, which would be used in art for the 1895, 1896, and 1897 calendars, and on others until the year 1903. The young women depicted on these calendars held glasses of Coca-Cola secured in these ornate holders. Today, original trademarked glass holders are very scarce and, as such, are highly desirable to collectors.

There is no known Coca-Cola Calendar for the year 1893, but it is certainly possible that there was one produced. With calendars having been issued for the two previous years, the absence of knowledge of yet another for this year is undoubtedly due to the lack of one having been found. Such is the romance and intrigue of searching for old advertising! As time goes by, new treasures, previously unknown to exist, are found in the field of historical Coca-Cola advertising. Old attics, trunks, and a variety of other unusual locations provide newly discovered rarities with each passing year. There have even been fabulous and rare pieces of advertising found inside the walls of old homes—items used as insulating material. It is truly amazing how and where historical items turn up!

Other advertising firsts which occurred in the early 1890s included the use of clocks for advertising Coca-Cola. Several documents in the Coca-Cola Archives also refer to 1893 as the first year when an enameled metal advertising sign was used. This is obviously different from the first metal or tin sign that was referred to as having been used in 1890. The reference to use of such signs is documented in *The Black Book*, which recounted *The History of Coca-Cola*. It states that "Enameled metal signs, being impervious to the weather were used chiefly in choice permanent locations." A large, colorful wall sign promoting Coca-Cola, painted on the side of the Young and Mays drug store in Cartersville, Georgia, appeared in 1894. Soon, such wall-painted signs would appear on buildings throughout the country.

Advertising expenses for The Coca-Cola Company increased from $12,393 in 1893 to $18,538 in 1894. This was a huge investment in promotion for a company whose total sales for 1894 were $88,910. Promotion of Coca-Cola at soda fountains quickly grew beyond the bounds of Georgia and the South. Wolf and Company, of Philadelphia, was a printer whose specialty was to produce printed advertising and promotion materials. The owner of that company notified Coca-Cola Company management that their product was widely available in Philadelphia, and that many prominent soda fountains were displaying advertising matter promoting it. By 1895, Coca-Cola was available in most parts of the country.

While Asa Candler envisioned Coca-Cola as a soda fountain drink, one of his customers saw things differently. Joseph A. Biedenharn, who sold Coca-Cola at his soda fountain in Vicksburg, Mississippi, was convinced that Coca-Cola would have success as a take-along drink at picnics and other social events. After having some success bottling Coca-Cola in 1894, the following year he began using a bottle design known as the "Hutchinson bottle" to hold carbonated Coca-Cola. This design had a permanent stopper affixed in the neck of the bottle which, when pushed down into the bottle, allowed a customer to consume the beverage. Even after Biedenharn enjoyed some initial success with his concept, Candler remained uninterested in bottling his drink. Bottled Coca-Cola, however, would later play a crucial role in the success of The Coca-Cola Company. Calendars produced in later years would reflect advertising incorporating both glasses of Coca-Cola as well as bottles of the beverage.

The next known Coca-Cola Company calendar was produced in 1894. Unlike other 1890s calendars and those produced after the turn of the century, this one did not feature the likeness of a young woman. It was, instead, a large business calendar with tear-off pages and advertising copy. Currently, only one example of this calendar is known to exist.

A calendar promoting Coca-Cola was produced in 1895, although a complete example is not known to exist. Interestingly, colorful advertising calendars with attractive artwork were sometimes used to decorate homes in the early years of graphic advertising. Individuals who could not afford paintings or fine prints would simply cut-off the monthly tear sheets and frame them as pictures. Another common practice was to retain the pretty image, but cut-off the advertising portion of the calendar or sign. Sometimes, rare but impaired advertising signs from the turn of the century are found which have been cut down to fit into picture frames. At the time, virtually no one envisioned these pieces as having future value. How wrong they were!

By the mid-1890s, Coca-Cola was a well-established product, with new syrup production plants being built in Chicago and Los Angeles. 76,000 gallons of Coca-Cola were sold throughout the country. In 1896, the first Coca-Cola metal advertising serving trays were ordered. With artwork identical to that found on the 1897 calendar, it is unknown whether the trays referred to in historical documents were actually distributed in 1896.

1896 also witnessed the issue of another advertising calendar. Featuring the brightest and boldest artwork of any of the calendars issued to that date, it was produced in a 6-1/2" x 10-1/2" size, with small tear-off sheets on the bottom right corner—one for each month. The calendar featured an attractive young lady holding a glass of Coca-Cola and, like other calendars from this era, is exceedingly rare. This calendar included proven slogans as ad copy, such as "Cures Headache," "Delicious and Refreshing," and "At Soda Fountains 5¢." A cardboard sign was also produced that same year, with identical artwork. The same young woman's visage is also found on the first known Coca-Cola advertising celluloid bookmark.

The 1897 calendar depicted the image of a young woman seated next to a table, drinking a glass of Coca-Cola. As previously noted, the identical image is seen on what is now known as the first use of the metal advertising serving tray by The Coca-Cola Company. More than likely, the tray was distributed in the same year as the calendar. A paper sign was also issued with the same artwork.

One can get a glimpse of the dynamic growth of Coca-Cola as evidenced by sales activity in the Pacific states, where sales increased from 955 gallons in 1896 to 4,954 gallons in 1897. Although founded in the South, The Company's vision for the beverage led it to market Coca-Cola nationally when it was just a five-year-old enterprise. The Company also had employed a trained sales force by this time. The 1898 annual report of The Coca-Cola Company made reference to them by stating: "Our salesmen have become known everywhere in this Union as gentlemen in every respect, and have not only maintained the good name of the Corporation but have succeeded in making Coca-Cola a familiar and gracious name in all the land."

The sophisticated approach with which The Coca-Cola Company marketed its product to soda fountains in the 1890s is remarkable when one considers that historical events such as the Klondike Gold Rush in Canada and Alaska were just beginning. In 1898, America emerged as a world power with its declaration of war against Spain over Cuba. To most, the concept of a motor driven "horseless carriage" was still just a rumor. Sophisticated advertising and marketing strategies were yet to become a trademark of American business. That is, except for The Coca-Cola Company.

Biedenharn Candy Company Hutchinson-stoppered bottle, circa 1894, is thought to be the first bottle to contain the Coca-Cola product.

The 1898 calendar design followed the theme of the first calendars. An attractive young woman holding a glass of Coca-Cola was shown in a cameo picture surrounded by flowers and slogans such as "Delicious and Refreshing," and "Relieves Mental and Physical Exhaustion." At the bottom right, the calendar noted "At All Soda Fountains 5¢." The same image as that used on the 1898 calendar also appeared on a bookmark. The *Black Book* history of The Company states that "the subject of calendars did not receive annual attention until 1898." It can be reasonably implied from this statement that calendars were not considered a to be a permanent part of the Coca-Cola merchandising program until that point.

We know that examples of Coca-Cola Calendars for the years 1891, 1892, 1894, 1895, 1896, 1897, 1898, and 1899 exist. That leaves only the years 1890 and 1893 for which there are no known examples. It is very likely that there was a calendar issued in 1893, but none have been located. Another distinct possibility is that such small quantities of these early calendars were issued that no remaining examples exist. For the known issues of any of the 1890s calendars, only a handful exist in any condition.

At this point in the firm's history, bottled Coca-Cola was not yet officially marketed. Several individuals were experimenting with methods to bottle soda waters of all kinds, but they remained the fledgling efforts of entrepreneurs. The early success of The Coca-Cola Company was based entirely on the sale of syrup sold to soda fountains by jobbers. But that was about to change. A monumental event in the historical development of The Coca-Cola Company occurred in 1899, when two lawyers—Benjamin Franklin Thomas and Joseph Brown Whitehead, both of Chattanooga, Tennessee—also took an interest in the concept of bottling Coca-Cola. They met first with Asa Candler in an unsuccessful attempt to gain bottling rights to the beverage. After further discussions, Candler agreed to give them sole bottling rights for Coca-Cola in most areas of the United States. The only exception to their territories were a few New England states and select areas of Texas and Mississippi. Shortly after concluding their agreement, the first officially sanctioned bottling of Coca-Cola began in 1899.

The arrangement between these two lawyers and Candler was quite simple: They would purchase syrup from The Coca-Cola Company and subsequently bottle it. Although it would appear that Candler himself lost a significant opportunity in this arrangement, he would benefit greatly from it in time because he retained exclusive control over, and sales rights for, the syrup itself. Thus, the relationship of the parent company (The Coca-Cola Company) and the regional bottlers began. Thomas and Whitehead had somewhat different ideas about how the business should be run, and they split their franchise areas into two regions blanketing the United States. Thomas assumed most of the North and East, along with the Pacific Coast, while Whitehead assumed the deep South and Southwest, Midwest, and areas to the Pacific Coast. These two enterprises then began to function as parent bottlers.

The two original parent bottlers later established smaller regional bottlers in their territories, including Western Coca-Cola bottling in Chicago, The Coca-Cola Bottling Company in Atlanta, and The Coca-Cola Bottling Company in Dallas. These regional bottlers were added just after the turn of the century. In turn, the regional bottlers added many other local bottlers and, by 1909, Coca-Cola had 379 bottlers throughout the United States. Thus, the foundation of a distribution network was firmly established—a network which would assure The Company's continued growth and expansion.

Within this system, the function of The Coca-Cola Company of Atlanta was twofold: First, to provide promotional direction for the merchandising of Coca-Cola. Second, The Company retained control of syrup sales to bottlers and to jobbers, who, in turn, serviced the fountain service business.

Joseph Brown Whitehead, of Chattanooga, Tennessee—one of the three founders of The Coca-Cola Company.

As fountain sales continued to boom, the bottling business took off as well. The original Hutchinson bottles used from 1895-1901 were replaced by bottles that could be sealed with a metal cap. Further, the bottled beverage would become a focus of Coca-Cola calendar advertising shortly after the turn of the century.

By 1899, The Coca-Cola Company increased its annual spending on advertising to $48,000—a figure that would double in the year 1900. The Company, from its inception, wanted to control the images, slogans, and advertising design wherever its product was sold. Consequently, The Coca-Cola Company produced an enormous amount of advertising collateral, and made it readily available to its fountain service customers and bottlers. 1899 was also the year when the first window display appeared. Shortly thereafter, colorful displays of advertising art dominated the windows of soda fountains, where advertising calendars, serving trays, signs, and beautiful cardboard cutout displays could be seen. Promotional clocks and porcelain dispensing urns were also used as premiums.

Advertising glasses were also part of the promotional effort made by The Coca-Cola Company, and early calendar issues showed the Coca-Cola logo proudly displayed on glasses held in metal holders. Later glasses were distributed in a fluted design that also displayed the Coca-Cola logo, and which had a line on the lower portion of the glass, indicating the level to which the fountain service should fill the syrup (the remaining area was to be filled with carbonated water). The importance of these early advertising glasses as a promotional tool is demonstrated by repeated reference to them in the firm's early historical documents.

The *Black Book* history of The Coca-Cola Company provides some insight into how the firm employed every promotional opportunity to increase its brand name recognition. Referencing the use of advertising glasses as promotional items just before the turn of the century, the book states that "The salesmen, in addition to Coca-Cola, were expected to sell bell shaped, eight ounce tumblers with the trade mark etched or enameled on the side of the glass and graduated for one ounce of Coca-Cola syrup. Orders for these glasses were taken in three and six dozen lots and for full barrels. Occasionally orders for as few as one dozen were sometimes accepted. The barrel lots were sold chiefly to jobbers. Considerable sales resistance was encountered, the dealer professing reticence to buy a commodity bearing an advertisement. This particularity applied to nickel plates, metal holders for glasses that were also for sale, and in the framework of which the trademark Coca-Cola was placed. However, considerable success attended the efforts of The Company in selling glasses and holders."

Three variations of Coca-Cola calendars were issued in 1899. Although different, they all had one important visual element in common: For the first time, The Company used art featuring a celebrity to promote its product. Hilda Clark, a prominent actress and singer of the day, was retained as a model. As is noted in the book, *Classic Coca-Cola Serving Trays*: "Without a doubt, Hilda Clark, proved to be the queen of Coca-Cola advertising for all time. Her likeness was featured on ten serving and change trays in addition to calendars, signs, a glass change receiver, cardboard posters, clocks, free drink tickets, bookmarks, trade cards, and other advertising items. Hilda's image was even used on an advertising poster which promoted Coca-Cola Chewing Gum. While she was featured for just five years (1899 to 1904), the use of her image in Coca-Cola advertising was prodigious."

Two of the 1899 calendar versions were identical in size (7-3/8" x 13"), while the third was 7-1/4" x 12-3/4". All three featured a cameo of Hilda Clark in the center, sitting at a writing desk with pen in hand. Two of the calendar designs used a format found on many early advertising calendars. Instead of having large-sized, tear-off pages stapled to the bottom of the calendar, small images of each full month were actually printed on the calendar.

1890s Hutchinson-stoppered bottle, featuring the famous script logo.

The other version featured the larger tear-off sheet design. The same art also appeared on a rare tin sign and a bookmark in 1899. Of course, the existence of three different versions of the 1899 calendar raises the question of whether, perhaps, there were more versions and styles of calendars for other years in the 1890s.

Beginning in 1896, The Coca-Cola Company used its preferred artwork—an attractive young lady—on a wide variety of advertising items each year. To provide a consistent image, a variety of objects such as celluloid bookmarks, serving and change trays, celluloid-covered note pads, menus, signs, posters, and, of course, calendars, displayed the identical artwork. By the turn of the century, the same image could be seen on many different advertising pieces. Some collectors select a favorite annual image, and display all of the various pieces that feature matching art. Assembling a collection of a calendar, serving and change tray, signage, and other related pieces bearing the same artwork from the early years could provide an expensive and challenging venture. The result of developing such a collection would be a fascinating and attractive display with historical significance.

Although Asa Candler was a big thinker, he had little concept of the full potential for his soft drink. When The Company moved into its new three-story offices in Atlanta in 1898, Candler proudly stated that the new building would be adequate for the needs of The Company for "all time to come." Advertising materials were an important asset of The Company. A large area of the third floor of the building was committed to storing and packing them. They were conveyed to the first floor via one of the first elevators installed in the South. Imagine if time travel were possible! Today's collector would find Nirvana sifting through the boxes of calendars, signs, serving trays, posters, and advertising promotional items in that historic building! In just a few short years The Company quickly outgrew Candler's edifice that was originally designed to serve the enterprise for "all time."

By the turn of the century, Coca-Cola Company sales extended far beyond every state in the Union, and the soft drink was being sold and marketed in numerous foreign countries. The year 1900 was a monumental year in many respects. Technological progress was moving forward at a rapid pace. The process of transmitting human speech via radio waves was discovered. That same year, the first flight of the Zeppelin dirigible occurred. The industrial revolution ushered in the dramatic growth of American cities, where workers were hired to produce a wide variety of products, many of which were transportation related. This period also witnessed the development of the food packaging industry. All sorts of canned fruits, vegetables, and meats became commercially available. In just a few short years, The Coca-Cola Company had gone from packaging its syrup in jugs and crude barrels to a sophisticated bottled soft drink. The timing for The Coca-Cola Company, with its newly bottled Coca-Cola product that could be purchased in stores, was perfect. At the same time, soda fountains were continuing to flourish.

1899 embossed tin sign, featuring the image of Hilda Clark seated at a desk, with pen in hand, enjoying a Coca-Cola. This sign measured 20" x 28".

1891 YOUNG GIRL WITH TENNIS RACKET
6-1/2" x 9" • type A
Printed by Calvert Litho
PCA005.001

Notice the unusual type style used in place of the Coca-Cola logo. Because these calendars are both stock calendars that had to be imprinted, a different type had to be used. As you can readily see, Coca-Cola was not the only product advertised by Asa Candler in 1891.

1891 YOUNG GIRL WITH ROSES

6-1/2" x 9" • type A
Printed by Calvert Litho
PCA005.000

This is thought to be the first calendar to advertise the Coca-Cola product. Both examples shown here are "stock" calendars—pre-printed calendars that advertisers could later have imprinted with their company name and other information. Compared with the high cost of customized designs, this was a much less expensive way to purchase calendars.

1892 GIRL WITH BUTTERFLIES AND BIRDS

6-1/2" x 9" • type A
PCA006.000

This is also a stock calendar; however, it is possibly the first calendar to feature the Coca-Cola script logo. Coca-Cola calendars prior to 1900 are considered extremely rare.

1896 LADY WITH BIRDS

6-1/2" x 10-1/2" • type B
PCA101.000

The image of this lady can also be found on a large paper sign, a larger calendar, a hanging sign, and a bookmark, as well as other pieces. Interesting to note: There is no known existing example of the glass she is holding.

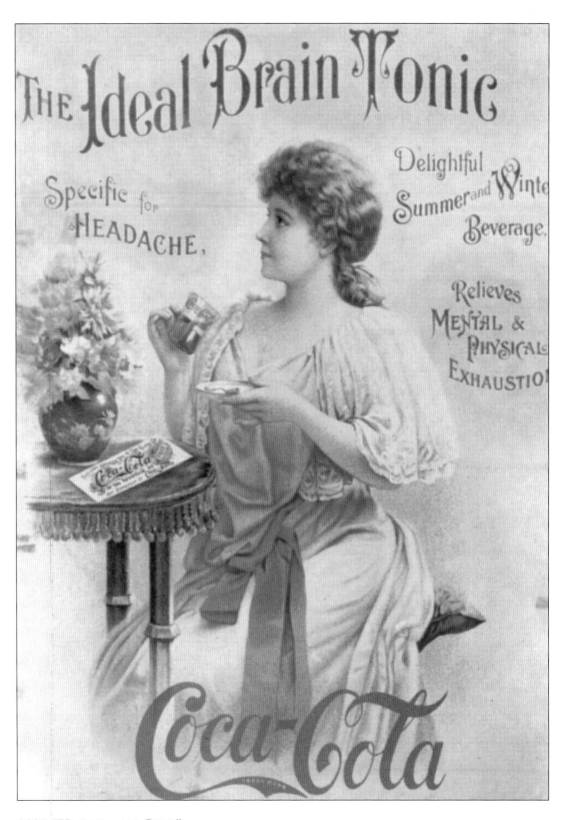

1897 "VICTORIAN GIRL"
7-1/2" x 13" • type B and C
PCA011.000

The image of the Victorian Girl can be found on at least two different examples of the 1897 calendar, as well as on tin signs, cardboard signs, serving trays, and other advertising material.

1898 GIRL WITH BLUE DRESS, AT TABLE

7-1/2" x 12-3/4" • type C

PCA012.002

There are three variations of this calendar. This beautiful and striking image was also used on tin signs, a cardboard sign, bookmarks, and other advertising of the time.

1899 HILDA CLARK—1

7-3/8" x 13" • type C •
"Published By Wolf & Co., Phila." in lower right corner.
PCA013.002

Hilda Clark was a very popular personality of the day. This is the first of her images used in Coca-Cola advertising. It was also used on tin and paper signs, serving trays, bookmarks, and many other advertising pieces. This calendar can be found in three variations.

CALENDARS OF THE FIRST DECADE OF THE TWENTIENTH CENTURY

Two calendar issues are known to exist for the year 1900. Both featured Hilda Clark, seated at a table holding a glass of Coca-Cola. While the two issues measure 7-1/4" x 12-1/4", the design of each of the calendars is quite different. One has monthly tear sheets located on the lower half of the calendar, while the other features small vignettes at the top and the bottom for each month of the year. Now familiar slogans such as "Cures Headache," "Relieves Mental and Physical Exhaustion," and, of course, "Delicious and Refreshing," appear on both calendar issues. The Company had specific messages it wanted to associate with its soft drink, and these went beyond simply quenching thirst. The same art, featuring Hilda Clark, was also displayed on both the 1900 serving and change trays.

Although not large in the context of the value of today's dollar, The Coca-Cola Company's advertising expenditure of $84,000 in the year 1900 resulted in many calendars, signs, serving and change trays, posters, and even paintings on the outside of buildings. We know, from records obtained from the Coca-Cola Archives, that metal serving trays cost The Company just over a nickel apiece just after the turn of the century. Calendars were even less expensive, costing in the neighborhood of two cents each.

In 1901, the bottling business was taking off. Thirteen bottlers were established by the end of the year. From that point on, the number of bottlers multiplied dramatically. Still, artwork advertising Coca-Cola in a bottle is not known to exist prior to 1903, when a serving tray, featuring a bottle as the central image, was issued.

Other world events in 1901 were to play an important role in the development of American business. Daimler, in Germany, produced its first complete Mercedes automobile. The first motorized bicycle was also successfully produced. Soon, the horse and buggy would lose out to the superiority of motorized transportation for personal travel and commerce. Following a century of steam power, the age of electricity was under way. Other important historical developments were rapidly changing the United States and the world—many of which would help propel distribution and marketing of the Coca-Cola soft drink.

With its valuable merchandising role clearly established, the Coca-Cola calendar continued to share a major role, along with the metal serving tray, as an effective advertising tool. Convinced of the versatility of the advertising calendar, The Company elected to produce an annual issue with new art. Two calendar issues are known to exist for 1901. One, measuring 7-3/8" x 13", features a young girl, seated at a table with a vase of flowers, and holding a glass of Coca-Cola. The second issue bore the image of Hilda Clark in a 7-5/8" x 11" format, surrounded by colorful flowers against a deep wine-colored background. Both had tear-off sheets for each month of the year stapled to the lower half of the calendar. The artwork of Hilda Clark was also featured on the 1901 serving and change trays. Early advertising pieces such as these are true treasures.

The Coca-Cola Company generated significant cash revenues early in its history. Sensing that advertising was a key to expanding its markets, Coca-Cola spared no expense in the development of promotional pieces. The finest illustrators were used to create images pleasing to the firm's management. Candler, a deeply religious man, avoided images of scantily clad young women in art. Instead, he preferred wholesome, attractive models who embodied the image of the pretty girl next door. Most were anonymous models who had a look that

Chapter 3

The Company wanted to portray. Over the years, the images of these young women chronicled the many changes in fashion and styles in our society. In today's somewhat jaded age, having an early calendar hanging on the wall offers an opportunity to view a most pleasant image of history, depicting an innocent time long gone by.

Finding early calendars with wonderful Coca-Cola advertising art is difficult to say the least. Most of the existing examples are firmly held in the hands of advanced collectors. Occasionally, such pieces are offered for sale through antique advertising auctions or catalog sales. When they are, the competition for high quality pieces is brisk, with many individuals seeking to add them to collections. Over the years, Coca-Cola advertising art has also proven to be an outstanding investment. Early calendars, which were sold for a few hundred dollars in the 1970s, now bring five figures. And, the future appears to be equally as bright!

The year 1902 saw the release of yet another Coca-Cola calendar. Perhaps there were additional versions, but at this point in time, only one design is known to exist. Featured in a 7-1/2" x 14-1/2" size, the calendar bears the image of a very young girl holding a glass of Coca-Cola. Tear sheets for each month were attached to the bottom half of the calendar. Wolf and Company Litho produced this and many of the other early Coca-Cola calendars and paper posters. The same image was also used on a menu in 1902.

In 1903, The Coca-Cola Company is known to have produced two different calendars, which were in most respects very similar. Both featured the same pose of Hilda Clark holding a glass of Coca-Cola, and both were produced in a 7-3/4" x 15" size. The only real difference in the two is a variation of the logo. Hilda Clark was popular with The Coca-Cola Company in 1903. Her image is seen on several serving and change trays, bookmarks, menus, and other advertising items issued that same year.

The Coca-Cola Company ventured further into the advertising world in 1903. The first Coca-Cola magazine advertisement appeared in a publication called *Munsey's*. Also, in keeping with the latest developments in transportation technology, The Company purchased its first motorized vehicle to be used as an advertising truck. Certainly the use of delivery vehicles adorned with innovative advertising could be the subject of a book in and of itself. The Company also held its first convention in 1930, which was attended by 29 salesmen.

1904 represented a hallmark year for The Coca-Cola Company. Sales exceeded one million gallons for the first time. There were 123 bottlers throughout the United States, and some 356 jobbers delivered syrup in containers to soda fountains. Owing to the growing significance of the bottling operations, a label specific to the Coca-Cola bottle was registered with the U. S. Patent Office.

The year 1904 was also one of notable historic importance. Theodore Roosevelt, later to be recognized as one of America's truly great leaders, was elected President of the United States. The first telegraphic transmission of photographs was achieved. Work on the Panama Canal commenced, and the Rolls-Royce Automobile Company was founded. All of these

1903 embossed tin sign, featuring Hilda Clark. This sign measures 15" x 18-1/2".

developments proved positive for The Coca-Cola Company. A more mobile society was becoming increasingly exposed to the delicious and refreshing soft drink known as Coca-Cola.

That same year, Lillian Nordica became the second famous celebrity to be featured as a subject on Coca-Cola Company promotional advertising. Her image was first used on the 1904 calendar, a paper sign, and on other pieces as well. Lillian Norton (Nordica was her stage name) was born in 1857, in Farmington, Maine. While a teenager, she developed a superb soprano voice. Her family sent her to Europe to study music in the 1870s and 1880s. While in Europe, she made her debut in concert and on stage. Her first major appearance in America was in 1877, at Madison Square Garden, as a soloist. From there, she toured Europe and achieved acclaim as an accomplished vocalist.

A natural extension for Nordica, in light of her world-class talent and stature as a singer, was the stage. After appearances in Europe, she made her first stage appearance at the Metropolitan Opera House in New York in 1890, where she portrayed Leonora in "IL Travatore." Nordica continued her career as a singer and stage actress until 1913, when she appeared in a recital at Carnegie Hall. Shortly thereafter, she died on May 10, 1914. *Groves Dictionary of Music and Musicians* says of Nordica: "She excelled both in dramatics and singing, but was a better singer than actress."

The 1904 calendar image is attributed to Lillian Nordica. A picture, located in The Coca-Cola Company Archives, shows her in a pose nearly identical to the one seen on the calendar. Issued in a 7-3/4" x 15-1/4" size, the calendar depicts the subject, wearing an elegant dress, standing next to a table with a glass of Coca-Cola on it. As would continue to be the design for the future, the calendar had tear-off pages for each month on the bottom half of the calendar. Both bottle- and glass-art examples of this calendar are known to exist.

A second, and much more unusual, calendar design for the year 1904 has surfaced, as well. Although it is believed that the Lillian Nordica calendar was the primary issue used to promote Coca-Cola throughout the country, another calendar design for the same year featured very different artwork. Undoubtedly purchased in very small quantities, this calendar features the image of a very young girl wearing an ornate straw hat. The same artwork was used on a calendar in two versions—marking the first year in which this was done. One version promoted bottled Coca-Cola, and the other version promoted a fountain glass serving. Both versions are exceedingly rare, and both were issued in a 8-1/4" x 15-1/4" size, with monthly tear off pages. The copy at the bottom of the "bottle" version of the calendar made reference to both carbonated Coca-Cola in bottles, as well as Coca-Cola at soda fountains.

While young attractive women were the primary subjects of Coca-Cola art, The Company did use images of children and adults in magazine advertisements developed

This 8-1/2" x 11" glass-covered cardboard sign from 1904 had an elegant and ornate metal frame with a chain hanger. It features the image of Lillian Nordica, and is sometimes referred to as the "Red Artwork."

by the Massingale Agency during this same period. Later, the images of children were also seen in calendars during the 1930s.

By 1904, it was clear that advertising for Coca-Cola was expanding its marketing focus beyond the soda fountain. With more and more bottling plants coming on-line, advertising depicting bottles was beginning to surface. Over the ensuing years, The Company issued numerous calendars in two versions. Each set featured identical artwork, the versions differing only in depicting either a Coca-Cola bottle or a soda fountain glass. Years in which both bottle and glass versions were produced included 1904, 1908, 1914, 1915, 1916, 1917, 1919, 1920, 1923, 1927, and 1928. It is very possible, however, that there were bottle art calendars issued for other years, as well. Most of the early calendars known to exist feature "glass art," since the primary market for Coca-Cola was the soda fountain, but in recent years, "bottle art" versions of these calendars have also surfaced.

In 1905, Lillian Nordica's likeness was featured on a wide range of advertising art, including a calendar, serving trays (in both glass and bottle versions), signs, menus, free-drink tickets, advertisements in publications, bookmarks, and other items. The range of advertising collateral featuring her likeness would provide for a wonderful collection in and of itself. The 1905 calendar displaying Lillian Nordica's likeness was printed in a 7-1/4" x 15-1/4" size, with tear-off pages for each month located on the bottom half of the calendar. Since The Coca-Cola Company issued serving trays in 1905 featuring both bottle and glass art, it is very possible that they did the same with their calendars, but, to date, only calendars featuring soda glass art are known to exist. As with other calendars from the first decade of the twentieth century, the images on the 1905 calendar display deep and rich colors. As previously noted, the stone-litho process used to create these impressions required many different plates and separate press runs. Due to their beauty, it is no wonder that these calendars are so highly prized by advanced collectors.

In 1900, The Coca-Cola Company had spent $84,000 on advertising and promotional expenses, but by 1906, just six years later, that amount was increased to nearly a half a million dollars! The Company's philosophy was to have its soft drink product promoted in prominent places everywhere people went. The Secretary's report for 1906 accounted for expenditures of nearly $150,000 for painted wall displays and street car advertising alone. Wolf & Company, of Philadelphia, the firm which printed many of the early Coca-Cola calendars, paper signs, and other paper items, was the recipient of more than $55,000 of the 1906 Coca-Cola Company advertising budget. That same year, leather novelties, metal signs, Ingraham clocks, celluloid pieces, paper napkins, matches, thermometers, door plates, metal trays, pocket knives, and other various advertising objects were purchased by The Company for the advancement of its trademark.

The next issue of calendar art is known as the "Juanita" design. The name "Juanita" has been attributed by collectors to the calendar design, due to the existence of sheet music, entitled "Juanita," which bears an identical picture of the same young woman. Typical of what was done in this era, other items produced with this image included a serving tray, change tray, tin sign, hanging paper sign, and a pocket mirror—all of which were issued in the same year. The impetus for changing calendar artwork was undoubtedly due to the need to create something new and distinctive for each annual calendar issue. The 1906 calendar, which is extremely difficult to locate in any condition, was printed in a 7-3/4" x 14-1/4" size, with tear-off sheets on the lower half of the calendar for each month.

The calendar dated 1907 is referred to as the "Relieves Fatigue" design. The picture on this calendar, which is identical to the one on the 1907 serving and change trays, is of a lovely young lady holding up a glass of Coca-Cola. To the right of her visage is the copy "Relieves Fatigue 5¢." The beautiful auburn-haired woman in the "Relieves Fatigue" calendar is adorned in a lovely green dress, shown against a deep and beautiful purple background. It was printed in a 7" x 14" size, with tear-off pages for each month on the lower half of the calendar. Because of its feminine and seductive design, the art on this calendar resembles that used on some of the most desirable saloon advertising art of the day to promote beer, whiskey, and cigars. In addition to trays, other advertising pieces with the same design as the 1907 calendar include a pocket mirror, self-framed tin sign, and a cardboard sign. The calendar and signs are all exceedingly desirable and rare.

The 1908 calendar features yet another beautiful design. The artwork depicts a lovely young woman in a red dress, with brightly flowered matching red hat, drinking a glass of Coca-Cola. She is seated at a table, with a note in front of her that reads, in script: "Good to the last drop." This advertising slogan would later become a trademark slogan for a coffee company, and was used over a period of many years. Within the last couple of years, a version of this calendar surfaced with bottle art. Until that time, it was believed that only soda-glass art was produced for distribution. The calendar was printed in a 7" x 14" size, with tear-off pages on the lower half of the calendar for each month. A larger version is also known to exist. Art matching that of the 1908 calendar also appeared on a pocket mirror and two paper signs. No serving trays with similar art are known to exist.

In 1909, The Coca-Cola Company issued a new calendar design, which has since become known as the "Exhibition Girl" art. The artwork for this calendar was initially copyrighted in 1908, and subsequently was used in 1909. In this design, a young woman is seated at a table holding a glass of Coca-Cola. Behind her is a river, with gondolas in the water and illuminated buildings in the background. The rim is blue and gold, with four coca nuts distinctly highlighted. The slogans on the calendar are "Drink Coca-Cola" and "Delicious and Refreshing." As a departure in size from its predecessors, the 1909 calendar was issued in a larger 11" x 20-1/2" size. Continuing with a design feature used since 1901 and for all future company issued calendars, it had tear-off pages for each month on the bottom half of the calendar. The same design appeared on a pocket mirror, two serving trays, and a change tray.

The year 1910 marked a period of just 18 years since Asa Candler had incorporated The Coca-Cola Company. During those years, The Company achieved sensational growth while other emerging soft drink firms either floundered or, at best, grew much more slowly. While The Company had a winning product, its superior marketing and promotional strategies were clearly the difference. Coca-Cola had a comprehensive and detailed strategic plan. In 1909, The Company began to issue a publication entitled *The Coca-Cola Bottler*. While mostly containing information about equipment and the methods used to bottle Coca-Cola, it also provided insights into some of the promotional advertising pieces being distributed at the time. Today, issues of that publication contain some of the most extensive pictorial information about early Coca-Cola advertising.

The August 1909 issue of *The Coca-Cola Bottler* included a picture of the Coca-Cola Bottling Works in Rockford, Illinois. As was the case in other early photographs of Coca-Cola advertising displays, the calendar was in prominent display. Beyond that, the photograph demonstrates just how far the firm had come with its merchandising in just under twenty years of incorporation. The plant interior, although spartan, was adorned with oil cloth signs, the 1908 calendar, cherub cardboard cutouts, festoons, large metal signs, small metal signs, and a virtual plethora of Coca-Cola advertising art. It is obvious that early bottlers were very aware of their role in promoting the product.

With industry and business booming in the U. S. during the first decade of the twentieth century, employment opportunities were available for major segments of the population. Workers were now experiencing a new concept called "the weekend." With increased leisure and travel time, luxuries such as soft drinks, which provided a splendid opportunity for socializing, were growing in popularity. By 1910, sales of Coca-Cola syrup totaled 4.2 million gallons. Whether in a bottle or at a soda fountain, Coca-Cola was fast becoming available everywhere. The Coca-Cola Company benefited from this growing affluence of society. Having the "Delicious and Refreshing" drink at hand was not just for satisfying thirst, but, through creative imagery, had truly become *the* thing to do.

Calendars

1900 HILDA CLARK—2

7-1/4" x 12-3/4" • type C
"Published by Wolf & Co., Phila." in lower
right corner
PCA014.001

This second image of Hilda Clark can be found on three calendar variations, serving trays, tin and paper signs, bookmarks, and coupons.

1901 HILDA CLARK—3

7-5/8" x 11" • type D

"Photo copyright by Morrison Co. Chicago 1900" printed in lower center. "Published by Wolf & Co., Phila." printed in lower right.

PCA016.000

This artwork has also been referred to as "Hilda with Roses," and it was used on many pieces of advertising in 1901, including paper signs, serving trays, menus, a small celluloid-covered clock, and other objects.

1901 GIRL WITH PANSIES

7-3/8" x 13" • type B
"Copyrighted 1899 Wolf & Co., Phila." imprinted on edge
of table. This date refers to the copyright year of the artwork.
"Printed in Germany" in lower right corner.
PCA015.000

This is a colorful and attractive image of a young lady holding a very elegant fountain glass. It was also used on other
advertising in 1901, including a very beautiful paper sign.

1902 GIRL WITH FEATHERED HAT

7-1/2" x 14-1/2" • type D
"Copyrighted By Coca-Cola Co." in lower left corner of print.
"Published by Wolf
& Co. Phila." printed in lower left. "I Love Its Flavor" slogan
printed in script at lower right.
PCA017.000

An interesting note on this artwork is a book on the table in front
of the model, printed with the name of Coca-Cola branches. It is
not large enough to accommodate all of the names. New York and
Boston are actually printed on the table itself. The image of this
very stylish young lady also appears on a paper sign, menu, and
other advertising from 1902.

1903 HILDA CLARK—4

7-3/4" x 15" • type D
"Copyrighted 1902 By Coca-Cola Co"
printed in lower left. "Published by Wolf
& Co. Phila." printed below.
PCA018.000

This calendar can also be found with a 1901 copyright
date, with a logo variation. This final image of Hilda
Clark was used extensively by Coca-Cola on a series of
serving trays, paper and cardboard signs, menus, peri-
odical advertising, a celluloid clock, and other objects.

**1904 LILLIAN NORDICA
(RED ARTWORK)**

7-3/4" x 15-1/4" • type D
"From photo copyright by DuPont 1903
published by Wolf & Co., Phila." printed
in lower right.
PCA019.000

This is the first of two images of Lillian
Nordica, a famous opera singer of the period. An envelope on the table bears her
name. This calendar has been dubbed the
"red artwork version," for obvious reasons.
This calendar was also produced in another
version, which also shows a paper-label bottle on the table and the additional words
"Carbonated in Bottles" on the oval sign.

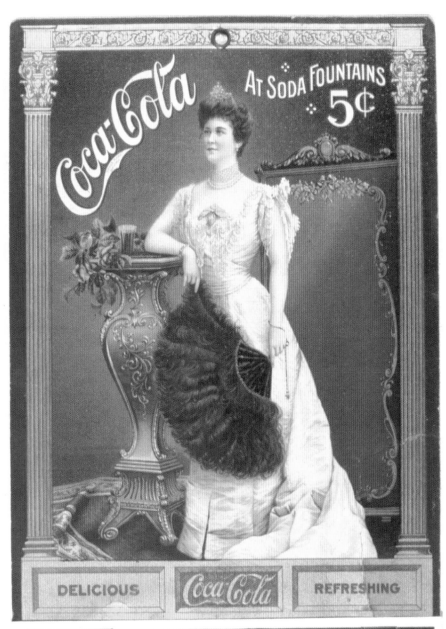

1905 LILLIAN NORDICA
(GREEN ARTWORK)

7-3/4" x 15-1/2" • type D
"From photo copyright by Dupont 1904"
printed in lower left. "Published by Wolf
& Co. Phila." printed in lower right.
PCA020.000

This second image of Lillian Nordica, dubbed
the "green artwork version," was also used on
many cardboard, paper, and tin signs; serving
trays; bookmarks; and many other advertising
pieces.

1906 "JUANITA"

7-3/4" x 14-1/4" • type D
"From Painting copyright 1905 by Wolf & Co.
Phila." printed in lower left.
PCA021.000

The artwork has been dubbed "Juanita" by collectors
because this image also appeared on sheet music
titled "Juanita." The image seen here was also used
on cardboard signs, serving trays, a small celluloid
clock, and other objects.

1907 GIRL WITH GREEN DRESS, HOLDING GLASS

7" x 14" • type D
"From painting copyright 1906 by Wolf & Co., Phila." printed in lower left.
PCA022.00

This classic and very popular image has been dubbed "Relieves Fatigue" by some collectors because the artwork bears that slogan. The same girl can be found on serving trays and tin signs. A larger version of this calendar was also printed.

1908 LADY IN RED, AT SODA FOUNTAIN

7" x 14" • type D
"Painting only copyrighted by Wolf & Co. 1907"
printed in lower left.
PCA023.00

A variation of this calendar can be found with a paper-label bottle on the table. A much larger version exists, as well. It is sometimes called the "Good To The Last Drop" calendar because a card on the table carries that slogan. This outstanding piece of artwork can also be found on paper and cardboard signs, as well as on other advertising.

1909 "EXHIBITION GIRL"

11" x 20-1/2" • type F

PCA024.000

"Copyright 1909 by The Coca-Cola Co." printed in lower right corner of print.

Other images of this model can be found, with a solid red background, on cardboard signs. Notice the addition of a bottle on the pad, as well as the fountain glass.

CALENDARS OF THE YEARS 1910-1919

Over the years, The Coca-Cola Company retained a variety of artists and illustrators to produce its advertising images. The first known illustrator of note to be commissioned by The Company was Hamilton King, who was best known for his colorful depiction of the "Gibson Girl" look. His subjects, often wearing colorful hats, projected a flamboyant look that was popular at the time. Calendars for the years 1910, 1911, 1912, and 1913 featured his art.

The 1910 Hamilton King art calendar was produced in a 8-3/4" x 17-1/2" format. The copy stated "Drink Delicious Coca-Cola." Also, in small print to the left of the picture, was the notation "The Coca-Cola Girl." Now it was not just a popular look promoting the product, but the look and the product had become one in the same in the form of the Coca-Cola girl. King's art focused on the colorful hat and the girl's face. The same image was used for the 1910 serving tray, change tray, and a pocket mirror.

Still another calendar design was issued for 1910, which did not feature Hamilton King art. A favorite of advanced Coca-Cola calendar collectors, it has become known as the "Happy Days" calendar, due to the text which is printed below an attractive young lady. Just below her visage is bold copy, which states: 'Happy Days' Drink Coca-Cola. It is unclear why The Company issued two calendar designs for the same year. The "Happy Days" calendar was featured in a 15" x 26" large format, which was a precursor to the larger calendars that would follow in years to come. This is another very scarce calendar that is much sought after by collectors.

In 1911, The Coca-Cola Company reached another high water mark in its history by allocating one million dollars for advertising and promotion. The 1911 calendar again featured Hamilton King art. Produced in a 10-1/2" x 17-3/4" size, the calendar depicted another of the "Coca-Cola Girl" art designs, with a flower-covered hat and the face of the girl providing the primary focus of the art. Hamilton King had a look and style of art unlike that of his contemporaries. It was light, airy, and interpretive, as opposed to most Coca-Cola advertising images, which were more realistic in appearance, with models shown in basic poses. King was an illustrator for numerous periodicals of the time, and his primary subject was pretty young ladies.

Two varieties of Hamilton King art calendars were issued in 1912. The 1912 calendars, unlike the Hamilton King calendars issued in 1910, 1911 and 1913, which focused on the face of the model, depicted a full figure of a young woman drinking a glass of Coca-Cola. In a loose and impressionistic style, the silhouette of the fashionable young woman appears as the central focus of the artwork. One version was produced in a 9-3/4" x 19-1/4" size, which featured ad copy on the lower portion of the calendar, just above the monthly tear sheets. The second, and larger, version was produced in a 12-1/4" x 30-3/4" size which had the same image as the smaller design, but which also had ad copy at the top of the calendar as well as just above the calendar pages.

Just as designs on Coca-Cola advertising were changing, so, too, was the world. The year 1912 was marked by several events that highlighted its chapter in U.S. history. Woodrow Wilson was elected President of the United States, and both Arizona and New Mexico achieved statehood. The very first parachute jump from an airplane was successfully executed in that year. But still another historic event took placed that has since been memorialized in books and movies. The world-class luxury liner Titanic tragically sunk on her maiden voyage, after colliding with an iceberg. This shocking tragedy resulted in the deaths of 1,513 people, including many of the rich and famous who paid large sums of money to be a part of the inaugural trip. At the same time, as affluence and modern means of transportation were becoming increasingly available to the masses, the dynamic advertising campaign of The Coca-Cola Company was proving highly effective in contributing to The Company's growth. Times and styles were, as ever, evolving and changing. This year, for the very first time, a swimsuit girl was featured in Coca-Cola advertising.

By 1913, the calendar had become a centerpiece of The Coca-Cola Company's promotional campaign. This is the first year for which an accounting exists relating to the number of calendars produced. *The Black Book: History of Coca-Cola* records that one million 1913 calendars were distributed. That same year, five million tin signs of all shapes and sizes were furnished to Coca-Cola jobbers, bottlers, and the general marketplace. A distinct advantage of the calendar was that it presented the opportunity to deliver different slogans and advertising messages on the same basic item. With twelve monthly calendar pages available, many issues presented a variety of slogans on the different monthly tear sheets, referring to the season of the year or to other promotional themes.

1913 was the fourth year in which Hamilton King art was used as the principal subject on The Coca-Cola Company calendar issue. Featuring a pretty young lady with a large flamboyant hat, the design was typical of the Hamilton King art of the period. The overall size of the calendar was 13-1/2" x 22-1/2". This same artwork was featured on cardboard cutouts, festoons, and serving and change trays.

Another calendar for 1913 has surfaced in recent years. One of the prettiest images in all of Coca-Cola advertising, this piece features art depicting a lovely young woman in a white dress, seated next to a white fence, and sipping bottled Coca-Cola through straws. This calendar was used by several of the bottlers. Photos from The Coca-Cola Company Archives show this same calendar used in displays by bottlers in the South, and one in Texas, indicating that the distribution was not limited to a single bottler. Since the art features Coca-Cola in a bottle, the design is considered a bottler issue. For years, only a handful of the top (picture of the girl) of this calendar existed, leading some to believe that these examples were paper signs rather than calendars. In recent years, however, an example of this art surfaced as a complete calendar. In all likelihood, the pieces thought to be paper signs were simply calendar tops that had been saved due to the beauty of the art. The 1913 bottler calendar was unique in another respect as well: The monthly pages ran from the mid-summer of 1913 through the summer of 1914. It was a large format calendar, having been issued in a 16" x 28" size.

For the 1914 calendar, Coca-Cola released a design that collectors now refer to as the "Betty" calendar—a designation earned by virtue of an advertising picture that displayed the same image, with

"Festoons" were elaborate cardboard cutout displays that adorned the backbars of many early soda fountains. This beautiful example, featuring a classic image of a beautiful woman enjoying a Coke, was painted by artist Hamilton King.

the name "Betty" printed below it. Since it was also accepted for calendar use, this particular image must have found favor with Coca-Cola Company sales and merchandising staff.

The January 1915 issue of *The Coca-Cola Bottler* contains an interesting history of another advertising piece that used the same artwork as the 1914 calendar. The most valuable piece of "Betty" advertising art today is the self-framed tin sign. Along with other "Betty" art pieces used to advertise Coca-Cola, this sign was issued in 1914. The following article, accompanied by a photo of the piece, was written to advise Coca-Cola bottlers about the availability of the sign and, as such, provides some interesting information on the use of "Betty" advertising art.

"In our last issue we referred to a new piece of advertising that is being given prominent display by Coca-Cola dealers.

"We are enabled, through the courtesy of the publishers at 'Printers Ink,' New York, to show a cut of a photograph of this sign. This cut was used in a recent issue of 'Printers Ink' to illustrate an article on "making sure dealer 'Helps' are used," in which article the writer refers to the Coca-Cola sign and says that 'obvious quality lessens waste.'

"As will be seen, this sign is a work of art. It is lithographed in fourteen colors, and the entire sign, including frame, is stamped from a single sheet of metal.

"The subject is 'Betty,' the 1914 calendar girl. It is said that the manufacturers made the dies for this sign at a cost of $6,000, and that it required many months to make it. The edition has been limited to 10,000 pieces.

"While we are not advised as to whether there will be a large enough supply of these portraits to equal the demand from all quarters, we suggest that any Coca-Cola Bottler who wants a distinctive piece of Coca-Cola advertising with which to adorn the wall of his office he will have to go quite a distance and spend considerably more than the cost of this sign to find a happier combination— a durable and beautiful piece of work. The sign measures over all, 32 x 44 inches."

Perhaps to some, a production quantity of 10,000 advertising signs appears to be a significant number. It is doubtful, however, that more than one percent of the original issue of these beautiful signs exists today in collections and/or historical archives. Of those that do remain, many exhibit considerable wear and fading, while only a precious few exist in nearly pristine condition. It is interesting to note that fourteen different colors were used to print the sign. It is also instructive to consider that The Company viewed this as art, and undoubtedly hoped the image would find favor with the public to the point that these advertising pieces would be used for decorative purposes. This large and impressive sign, along with other "Betty" art pieces, provides a glowing sentimental reminder of a bygone era. The fact that some examples survive to this day indicates they were appreciated as far more than an advertisement.

Until 1914, calendars were used primarily as promotional items in soda fountains and other commercial establishments. In 1914, The Coca-Cola Company, always the leader in developing and expanding its market, began offering calendars as a premium item to the public. A January 1914 ad in *The People's Home Journal* showed the image of "Betty"

Photo of a horse-drawn delivery wagon, taken in 1914. The nattily dressed driver not only delivered Coke and candy, but advertising material, as well.

along with an offer for a free calendar. To receive a calendar, the respondent was asked to simply "Write for 'Betty.' That's the name of the beautiful girl on the Coca-Cola 1914 Calendar. Send your name and address and a 2 cent stamp (it pays part of the postage) and we'll send you free and postpaid this beautiful reproduction of the oil painting 'Betty,' painted especially for us. 1914 calendar is attached. FREE Coca-Cola booklet enclosed. THE COCA-COLA CO. Atlanta, Ga."

The art on all but one advertising piece simply depicts the picture of "Betty," with copy in the right-hand corner reading, "Drink Coca-Cola, Delicious and Refreshing." However, there is one notable exception. A very limited number of the 1914 calendars show "Betty" holding a bottle of Coca-Cola. This variation of the primary 1914 calendar is many times more scarce than the regular calendar, and, as such, is prized by advanced collectors. All in all, the popular "Betty" art was used on two variations of the 1914 calendar, a variety of serving and change trays, a cardboard sign, and the self-framed tin sign. A reproduction of the Betty art calendar was produced in the last twenty years, and it has been offered by unscrupulous dealers as an original. There are differences in the size of the calendar, and the reproduction lacks the color depth and definition of the original, which was produced using the stone-lithography printing process.

1915 was another important year for The Coca-Cola Company. It its search for distinctive packaging, the curved and unique shape of the now-famous Coca-Cola bottle was designed and patented. The Company recognized at its early stages that packaging was important. This bottle design added further to the merchandising success of the brand. Today, it is one of the most recognized product symbols in the world.

At the same time, many changes were affecting American society. The Ford Motor Company produced its millionth automobile. Signaling the continued rapid expansion of communication, the first transcontinental phone call between New York and San Francisco was successfully executed. There was an ominous development, as well. Germany began its blockade of England, and initiated belligerent actions toward some of its neighbors in Europe. By 1916, the United States was drawn into World War I. Even in times of worldwide strife and chaos, however, The Coca-Cola Company found ways to prosper.

Several of the calendars produced during the teens exhibit spectacular artwork, and the 1915 calendar is among the most exceptional ever produced. The young woman, shown wearing a stunningly beautiful lace dress and holding a parasol, is portrayed against a waterfront scene to her left. As with the 1914 calendar, two versions of this same art were issued. The most common version shows the young woman holding a glass of Coca-Cola. The other version, which is very scarce, shows her holding a bottle. There was also a minor variation in the "glass" version of the calendar: One issue features a gray and red logo, while the other bears a red logo only. It is safe to assume that there must have been a great deal of interest and participation in The Coca-Cola Company's free calendar ad offer in 1914, because the same promotion was also offered in 1915, and again in 1917.

Another interesting artwork design was produced for advertising in 1915, and again in 1916, which related to the calendar issues for those years. These were attractive cardboard cutout pieces showing an image of an artist painting

A circa 1912 photo showing a Coca-Cola Company truck decked out in a fall leaf motif, with a cardboard cutout of a typical Coca-Cola girl displayed on the front grill and side door.

the calendar artwork for each of these years, with copy proclaiming "one of America's famous artists painting The Coca-Cola Calendar Girl." No documented information is known to exist confirming the identities of the artist or models used for these cardboard cutouts.

As was done in 1913, another bottler calendar was issued in 1915. Because only a handful of these calendars are known to exist, it is likely that they were purchased by a single bottler. Since there were hundreds of Coca-Cola bottlers by this time, undoubtedly other calendars with Coca-Cola advertising were produced for them. From time to time, previously unknown calendars are found bearing local bottler advertising which were not produced by, or with the authorization of, The Coca-Cola Company.

The standard calendar design for 1916 was also issued in Coca-Cola bottle and soda glass versions. Demonstrating that incorrect information can become accepted as true over the years, most collectors and dealers improperly refer to this as the "Elaine" calendar. The 1915 calendar was titled "Elaine," and, for some reason, that name has also been attached to descriptions of the artwork on the 1916 calendar, serving and change trays, a self-framed tin sign, and a pocket mirror. Clearly, the artwork for the 1916 calendar features a different model than the 1915 calendar, which was, indeed, titled "Elaine."

The actual artwork for the 1916 calendar is copyrighted as "Girl with a basket of Flowers." The image shows a pretty young woman sitting on a wicker table, holding a glass of Coca-Cola in her left hand. The "Elaine" designation for this calendar is incorrect. Instead, it should be designated by the title of the actual copyrighted artwork.

Yet another calendar was offered by The Coca-Cola Company in 1916—for a specific purpose. Featuring "Miss Pearl White" holding a glass of Coca-Cola, this small 8" x 15" calendar was used as a magazine insert piece. It was unique among Coca-Cola calendars in that it was seasonal, with only the months of July, August, and September presented below the picture of Pearl White. Produced in much smaller quantities than the regular calendar issue for the same year, it is considered rare today.

Following the outbreak of war in Europe in 1916, it was only a matter of time before the United States would be drawn into the war against Germany. Believing its own sovereignty threatened by Germany, the U.S. finally entered World War I in 1917. As a result of the war, sugar rationing was instituted, impacting the expansion of The Coca-Cola Company and its popular soft drink. Advertising expenses actually dropped for the first time in The Company's history. By 1918, these expenses totaled $883,000—only half the amount spent on promotion just two years earlier. There were further war-related restrictions on advertising. Metal serving trays and signage had been staples of The Company's advertising program dating back to before the turn of the century. Due to the war, however, metal use was placed on restriction, as it was in short supply and needed to support the war effort.

With restrictions imposed on the use of metal, paper sign and calendar advertising art became even more important to The Coca-Cola Company during the war. The last new issue of the serving tray during the teens occurred in 1916, when the production of metal signs was curtailed, as well.

Magazine ad from 1915 shows the image of "One of America's famous artists painting The Coca-Cola Girl calendar." This art was used again in 1916.

This paper die-cut window display piece depicts a typical image of the All-American, wholesome girl that The Coca-Cola Company so often featured on their advertising in the mid-Teens.

Continuing its campaign to make the calendar available in consumer's homes and at commercial businesses, the 1917 calendar pictured a young woman named "Constance," who was shown seated at a table with a sporting scene behind her. Two variations were produced. One showed her holding a glass, with a bottle on the table in front of her. Still another, and scarcer, variety shows her holding a glass in her hand, with another glass on the table, as well. Up until 1917, during most, but not all, years of The Company's early history, the art pictured on a given year's calendar was also featured on a serving tray. Such was not the case in 1917, due to the metal shortage.

By November 18, 1918, World War I had ended, but not without tragic loss of life. Transportation methods continued to modernize, with the first delivery of airmail between Chicago and New York City taking just over ten hours. Railroads traversed over 250,000 miles, and the population of the United States reached 105 million. That same year, a worldwide epidemic of influenza caused the deaths of 22 million people. In the midst of a tumultuous year, The Coca-Cola Company prospered, although sugar rationing and disruption in the world economy were impediments to achieving the growth levels that had been reached prior to the war.

The standard calendar issue for 1918 did not reflect the difficult times which faced the country. In line with the well-established pattern of Coca-Cola advertising art, the scene pictured on the calendar was one which evoked images of the good times. In a striking setting, one girl is seen standing and holding a glass of Coca-Cola, while another girl, seated next to the first, is holding a bottle. Depicted in the background is a beach scene, including a refreshment stand and bathers. There was no need to issue a separate version of this calendar for the bottler and fountain service markets—this one calendar covered both bases. Along with other standard calendar issues of the teen years, the 1918 issue is highly prized by collectors for its exceptional eye appeal.

Another Coca-Cola calendar, also bearing the 1918 date, has surfaced. Issued in a small 5" x 9" size, it features the likeness of June Caprice, and is considered to be a distributor calendar, given away in large quantities. The back of the calendar provides information about Miss Caprice. This small calendar is not nearly as difficult to locate as the standard-issue calendar for 1918.

The survival rate of early paper advertising is certainly the result of chance rather than plan. It is doubtful that the creators of this advertising artwork ever envisioned it being collectible or valuable. Furthermore, paper is not a durable material. Subject to fading, moisture damage, and being eaten by insects and mice, it is difficult to imagine how any of the early treasures and images of early paper advertising have survived the ravages of time. Most "finds" of early Coca-Cola advertising collateral, such as calendars, cardboard signs, and other pieces, have occurred more often as the result of chance. Original advertising calendars have sometimes been located in mailing tubes, in unused condition, in a long-forgotten corner of an attic or old country store. Occasionally, individuals enjoyed the artwork found on advertising pieces so much that they framed and displayed them in their homes. Early calendar tops have been found in old frames but, all too often, the image area has been cut down to accommodate the frame dimensions. The allure of the artwork of early advertisers is even more appealing when one realizes how amazing it is that any of these fragile treasures still exist today.

Nineteen nineteen was a momentous year in The Coca-Cola Company's history. Asa Candler, who had guided The Company from its very beginning, elected to reap the ultimate benefit of his genius and efforts. Candler sold his enterprise for $25 million to Ernest Woodruff and an investment group. Shortly thereafter, The Coca-Cola Company was incorporated in Delaware as a publicly held firm, with stock being offered and publicly traded. Although $25 million dollars may seem like an incredible bargain today, it was an enormous sum of money at the time. Candler left an established organization that was primed for dynamic growth. The best was yet to come!

Today, owning one of the pre-1920 calendars can be described as a moderately serious investment. The primary 1919 calendar issue would provide the centerpiece of a wonderful collection. Bearing the image of a lovely young woman, the calendar also depicts a scene of an early military airport, with bi-planes in the sky and men in military uniforms in the background. A rather unusual feature of the art is the presence of a large, brightly colored, and detailed knitting bag, which is featured below the main image. To many collectors, the artwork on the 1915, 1918, and 1919 calendars are among the most desirable of all produced by The Coca-Cola Company.

A second and smaller distributor calendar was also issued by The Coca-Cola Company in 1919. Featuring the likeness of cinema star Marion Davies, this calendar was produced in a small 6-1/4" x 10-1/2" format. Unlike the larger primary calendar issue for 1919, it is unclear whether this version was distributed nationally or regionally. Surviving specimens are scarce, and not at all easy to locate.

1910 HAMILTON KING ART—1

8-3/4" x 17-1/2" • type F

"Painting only copyrighted by The Coca-Cola Co. 1909" printed in lower left corner. "Published by Wolf & Co., Philadelphia" printed in lower right corner.

PCA026.000

This is the first of four pieces of art produced by artist Hamilton King for The Coca-Cola Company. His signature appears on the calendar, which also bears the title: "The Coca-Cola Girl."

1910 HAPPY DAYS

15" x 26" * type F

"Copyright 1909, by Coca-Cola Co." printed in lower left corner of print.

PCA025.000

Dubbed the "Happy Days" calendar because of the interesting slogan. This calendar has eluded collectors over the years. Thus far, this wonderful image has appeared only on the calendar, and it has not been seen on other advertising or promotional pieces.

1911 HAMILTON KING ART—2

10-1/2" x 17-3/4" • type F

"Published by Wolf & Co. Philadelphia" printed in lower left corner. "Painting only copyrighted by The Coca-Cola Co. 1909" printed in lower right corner.
PCA027.000

This is the second piece of art produced by artist Hamilton King. This calendar also shows his signature, and is titled "The Coca-Cola Girl." Note that this calendar has a metal strip at the bottom of the print, as well as at the top.

1912 HAMILTON KING ART—3

9-3/4" x 19-3/4" (small version) • type F
12-1/4" x 30-3/4" (large version)
"Painting only copyrighted by The Coca-Cola Co., 1910" printed in lower left. "Published by Wolf & Co., Philadelphia" printed in lower right.
PCA028.000

This is the third piece of art produced by Hamilton King, and it has a completely different look than the other images that he produced for Coca-Cola. His signature is also different--comprised in this case of a simple "HK" in a box. While the image is the same on both the large and small versions of this calendar, a logo appears at the top of the large version only, and a larger pad is used. Similar Hamilton King art was used on a trolley sign and other display pieces in 1912.

1913 BOTTLERS' CALENDAR

Girl with red bow on hat
16" x 28" • type F
PCA030.000

Between 1911 and 1914, a number of these "Bottler Calendars" were produced. In each case, the model is shown holding a paper-label bottle of Coca-Cola. The trademark, slogans, and advertising message were on each individual calendar page. These bottler calendars are hard to find.

1913 HAMILTON KING ART—4

13-1/2" x 22-1/2" * type F
"Painting only copyrighted by Wolf & Co., 1912" and "Printed in Germany" printed in lower left.

This is the last piece of art produced by Hamilton King for a Coca-Cola calendar. This painting also shows his signature, and the model is depicted holding the fountain glass that was in use at the time. The glass bears an arrow in the shape of a five, as in five cents. This image also appeared on a series of serving trays.

1914 "BETTY"
13" x 32-1/4" • type F
"Copyrite The Coca-Cola Company" in lower right of print.
PCA035.000

This calendar was produced in two variations: with bottle and without bottle. Note that an extensive alteration of the artwork—lowering of the arm and repositioning the hand—was needed to accommodate the bottle. The bottle version of the Betty calendar has turned up much less often over the years. It is also interesting to note that this calendar was printed on a textured paper, which is sometimes mistaken for canvas due to the look and feel of the paper.

1915 "ELAINE"
13" x 32-1/4" • type F
"The Coca-Cola Company" in lower left of print.
PCA036.001

The 1915 Elaine calendar was produced in a glass and bottle version. The model's arm had to be repositioned to accommodate the paper-label bottle. The Elaine calendar is certainly one of the most highly desired of all "Teens" calendars. There is also a logo variation of this calendar—as shown here, with gray with red outline—as well as one with an all-red trademark.

1916 GIRL WITH BASKET OF FLOWERS

13" x 32-1/4" • type F
"c. The Coca-Cola Company" at lower left,
under print.
PCA037.000

Both glass and bottle versions of this calendar were
produced. Unlike the 1914 and 1915 calendars, this
artwork required very little alteration to accommodate
the bottle. Both bottle and glass versions have turned
up equally over the years.

CONSTANCE

1917 "CONSTANCE"

13" x 31-3/4" • type F

"c. The Coca-Cola Company" in lower left of print.

PCA038.000

The 1917 calendar was produced in two variations. However, these variations do differ from the previous glass and bottle variations—in both cases, Constance is holding a glass in her right hand. On one calendar, another glass appears on the table. On the other calendar, a paper-labeled bottle appears on the table. Background images of spectators, and a couple playing tennis, make this calendar particularly interesting.

CONSTANCE

1918		JANUARY			1918	
SUNDAY	MONDAY	TUESDAY	WEDNESDAY	THURSDAY	FRIDAY	SATURDAY
		1	2	3	4	5
6	7	8	9	10	11	12
13	14	15	16	17	18	19
20	21	22	23	24	25	26
27	28	29	30	31		

1918 TWO LADIES AT THE BEACH

12-1/2" x 30-3/4" • type F
"c. The Coca-Cola Company" in lower left of print.
PCA039.000

The 1918 calendar is certainly the most desirable of all the "Teens" calendars. Pretty girls on the beach always rank as collector favorites. Not only is this a colorful and beautiful piece of art, but the background image of couples enjoying the beach contributes to a very interesting calendar. Notice that one girl is holding a glass, while the other is holding a bottle—thereby eliminating the need
for two variations.

1919 GIRL WITH KNITTING BAG

13" x 31-3/4" • type F

"Copyright The Coca-Cola Company" in lower left of border.

PCA040.000

The 1919 calendar was produced in two versions: glass and bottle. The bright colors and wonderful art make this an extremely desirable calendar. With World War I finally over, this artwork commemorates the end of the war and the boys coming home. The image depicts a pretty girl, waiting for her boyfriend, with a knitting bag and a partially knitted sweater in the foreground. Bi-planes in the background and arriving soldiers crossing the airfield complete this classic piece of art.

1926

Compliments of The Coca-Cola Company. Atlanta. Ga.

CALENDARS OF THE "ROARING TWENTIES"

The 1920s marked a colorful, exciting, and tumultuous time in American history. World War I—a recent and tragic memory—was now over, and prosperity bloomed throughout the country. In 1920, a prohibition against the purchase of alcohol became law with the adoption of the 18th Amendment to the U.S. Constitution. By 1921, the first commercial radio station in the United States began transmitting regular radio programs from Pittsburgh, Pennsylvania. At the same time, the population of the nation reached nearly 120 million. With the automobile fast emerging as the primary and preferred mode of transportation, the country was becoming increasing mobile. The timing for additional growth in the distribution of flavored sodas and beverages was ripe. A developing economy had sparked a growing work force, and this labor force had more disposable income to spend on an ever-expanding variety of consumer products and packaged goods. The Coca-Cola Company had survived sugar rationing and the limitations caused by the war, and by the 1920s, was poised to continue its dynamic expansion.

Calendars issued in the twenties continued to feature a lovely young lady as the primary focal point. Some issues also included interesting background art and activities. For example, the first calendar issue of the 1920s depicted a summer scene, featuring a young woman as the primary subject, with a golf course behind her. The 1920 calendar design was issued in two versions. One version showed the girl holding a glass of Coca-Cola; the other depicted her with a bottle. Both oval and rectangular serving trays were issued with identical artwork, and the last change tray was issued by The Company in this year.

As with all Coca-Cola art featuring the visages of young women to promote the product, the very latest styles of clothing were featured. Consequently, if one were to examine a complete collection of Coca-Cola calendars, one could easily survey the change in fashions as they unfolded from year to year. No other single advertising collateral item produced by The Company provides the detailed chronological look at progressing styles seen in the calendars. Serving trays also provided a fashion study, but the calendars produced after 1910 were in a larger format than the trays, and the calendars alone have been issued continuously through the decades, whereas serving trays ceased to be produced in the early 1960s.

The 1921 calendar was produced in a single version. The Company opted to issue a calendar that would serve the promotional needs of both the bottlers and the fountain service trade by depicting an image of a bottle on a table next to an attractive young woman in a garden scene. The woman is, of course, shown holding a glass of Coca-Cola. Calendars were sold to bottlers and the syrup distribution trade for $45 per thousand, or four and a half cents each! Quantities of calendars distributed during the 1920s and 1930s totaled as many as two and a half million pieces per year. On the surface, it is hard to imagine why these calendars are so scarce in today's antique advertising market. Conversely, when one considers that they were printed on inexpensive, low-grade paper, and the measures that would be needed to preserve and save these items, it is perhaps more of a mystery as to why *any* have survived the ravages of time. Artwork identical to that on the calendar was also produced on a rectangular serving tray.

Chapter 5

The 1922 calendar issue is a favorite of many collectors. The Coca-Cola Company's marketing genius was evidenced in its ability to use art that captured warm images associated with wholesome fun, enjoyment, and everyday life. The 1922 calendar depicts a pretty young woman sitting on the edge of a bleacher, sipping a glass of Coca-Cola, with a bottle of Coca-Cola beside her. Over her shoulder, and in the background, a baseball game scene is pictured. The intricate design of her lace dress is lovely, and reminiscent of that seen in several other calendars issued in the teens. This is a blue chip Coca-Cola advertising calendar, with appeal to both Coca-Cola advertising aficionados as well as baseball memorabilia collectors. Americana at its best! A rectangular serving tray was issued with identical artwork, but due to its smaller image size, it did not feature the baseball scene.

The 1923 calendar is an attractive one—with a young brunette pictured in party attire, holding a glass of Coca-Cola. A second version, with identical artwork, pictured her holding a bottle. The January month tear sheet of the calendar demonstrated the use of Coca-Cola slogans to promote the use of the soft drink year-round, with the slogan "Thirst Knows No Season."

That same year demonstrated The Coca-Cola Company's continued genius at finding innovative ways to sell and merchandise its products. One of the most significant developments was Coca-Cola's introduction of the six-bottle carton. This carton had built-in carrying handles, making it easy to carry to picnics, parties, and social events of all kinds. The Company actually hired employees to go door-to-door to sell Coca-Cola in the new carton. Armed with bottle openers, which they were happy to install in peoples' homes, these sales representatives proved to be an effective means for increasing sales. The new carton, and the aggressive new sales approaches, helped to create the home consumption market for Coca-Cola. Robert Woodruff had a vision based on his desire to make Coca-Cola available everywhere. With convenient carry-home cartons for the consumer, The Company had extended its marketplace again.

The bottler's list of advertising material for 1924 demonstrates the wide variety of collateral available to promote Coca-Cola. The Coca-Cola Company provided bottlers with advertising materials at cost, and even offered a co-operative advertising program which provided an allowance based on the previous year's sales, and which could be applied toward the purchase of new advertising materials. Many of the items listed below are difficult to locate today, yet they were inexpensive and commonplace when issued.

ADVERTISING MATERIALS	COST TO BOTTLER
Cardboard cutouts "Bathing girl"	.27&1/2 cents each
Panels (cardboard) Summer	.40 each
Cloth signs 21" x 60"	.22 each
Metal signs 20" x 28"	$182.50 per thousand
Metal Flange Signs 12" x 28"	$190.00 per thousand
Trays	$157.50 per thousand
Calendars	$47.30 per thousand

In 1924, The Coca-Cola Company placed a lengthy ad, which described The Company's history and status, in several business-related publications. It provided an interesting overview of how, and to what point, The Company had evolved. The Company estimated that "Two billion, three hundred million drinks of Coca-Cola are sold a year through 415,000 retailers." Also stated was the fact that more than 1,250 bottling plants were in place. Of that number, 300,000 retailers were supplied Coca-Cola in bottles, and 2,300 jobbers delivered syrup to 115,000 soda fountains. The product was also being sold in 27 foreign countries.

Further evidence of The Company's voluminous advertising campaign was a statement from the same prodigious ad, which read: "There are 20,000 Coca-Cola walls and bulletins in the Untied States. Three million pieces of window display signs and other dealer-help advertising are being distributed in 1924. Two and one half million 1924 calendars were given away. Coca-Cola's message is carried in millions of copies of magazines and newspapers."

The 1924 calendar, like several of the previous issues, depicted a young woman in a stunning dress, holding a glass of Coca-Cola. Behind her, the image of a lily pond with light shimmering across it, completed the scene. As with several other issues, a bottle of Coca-Cola was also included in the artwork so as to eliminate the need for separate issues for the bottler and the soda fountain trade. This is a particularly beautiful calendar when the original mint-fresh colors are present. Many of the early calendars that still exist exhibit some level of fading. It is very important to properly frame such pieces, and to place them in areas where they are not subject to intense sunlight, or to the direct effects of an artificial light source. This topic will be covered in a upcoming section, which discusses how to preserve historical paper. This same art was also displayed on a serving tray, magazine advertisement, needle case, and a cardboard cutout.

By 1925, the roaring twenties were in full swing. Women's clothing styles were less inhibited than in previous years. They featured straight dresses without a waistline, and skirts which rose above the knees. The automobile had taken over. With the growth of radio broadcasts, America was being exposed to yet another fertile source of advertising and promotion. Soft drinks of all kinds were increasing in popularity.

The 1925 calendar issue reflects the spirit of the day in its artwork. The image features a young woman holding a glass of Coca-Cola, while a bottle of Coca-Cola is positioned on a table at her left. She is adorned in a high-fashion dress, with a fox fur around her neck. In the background, people are discernible in a party setting. This artwork, which also appeared on the 1925 serving tray, a cardboard cutout, a needle case, and in magazine advertisements, has been referred to by collectors as the "Party Girl" art. In the early 1990s, an unscrupulous individual reproduced both this and the 1924 Coca-Cola calendar,

December 1924 ad from The Ladies Home Journal, *featuring the artwork used on the 1925 calendar.*

and has attempted to sell them as originals. Be aware that both of these reproductions vary in size from the originals, and the pad sheets of the reproductions are on white paper, as opposed to the originals, whose pad sheets were brown, with white lettering. Several other characteristics distinguish the originals from the reproductions. Collectors need not fear reproductions, but they must arm themselves with the knowledge needed to discern the "real thing" from the phony pieces.

Calendar art, as with other Coca-Cola advertising images, was chosen to represent the latest in styles, and this art always associated the soft drink with pleasant settings and surroundings. It is interesting, however, that with all of the available resources possessed by The Company during its first forty years, and up through the 1920s, famous artists were not generally used to produce the firm's celebrated art. Other than the Hamilton King art used on trays and calendars from 1910-1913, most Coca-Cola advertising art does not even include an artist's signature. It is safe to assume that most of the artists chosen by Coca-Cola and its advertising agencies were talented, but relatively obscure, illustrators of their day.

The 1926 calendar represented a significant departure from previous years in that the calendar art was not duplicated on the serving tray distributed that year. For most years from 1897-1925, the art images on calendars were also used in the production of metal serving trays. After 1925, however, that strategy changed. The serving tray issue for 1926, for example, featured art depicting a couple in a golfing scene. The 1926 calendar depicted a young woman seated at a table, with a tennis racquet sitting next to her. She is shown holding a glass of Coca-Cola, drawn from an accompanying bottle which is next to her.

The beautiful artwork of the 1927 calendar was used on three calendar variations. The young woman depicted on this calendar appears particularly lovely in an alluring—almost seductive—pose, holding a necklace in her left hand and a glass of Coca-Cola in her right. The most common of the three versions has an inset on the lower left corner of the picture area of the calendar, showing a full bottle of Coca-Cola. A second issue does not display the image of the bottle inset on the calendar. Still another smaller version used the same artwork as the first version, but in the area just below the picture, and just above the monthly pages displayed below, there is a vertical inset area where the name of the individual soda fountain or business could be imprinted. Most often, these examples are indeed found with the names of soda fountains on them. This calendar art was obviously targeted at the bottler market (the one with the inset bottle); the soda fountain trade (the one with just the glass); or a soda fountain or other business (imprinted with the business establishment's name).

The January 1927 issue of *The Red Barrel* provides some useful insights into the importance of calendars in the Coca-Cola merchandising program. On the inside cover of the bottler publication is a picture of both the regular 1927 calendar issue and the smaller dealer calendar. Accompanying the photo was the following statement: "A calendar works each day, and four and a half million Coca-Cola calendars are working for Coca-Cola dealers daily. Artistic, decorative and useful—they find homes where other advertising is not admitted." Then there is a specific reference to the smaller dealer calendar which reads: "A Calendar with the dealer's Imprint: Thousands of dealers purchased reproductions of the big 1927 calendar, with their own name and advertisement prominently displayed. These provide for a splendid local tie-up with the big calendar. The painting on both is by Renwick, and they are printed in thirteen colors."

Following the precedent set the previous year, the 1928 calendar was made in several different versions. All featured a young woman in a stylish gold party dress, seated in a chair next to a small table. The most common version is the larger-size calendar, which pictures the model holding a glass of Coca-Cola, with a bottle sitting on the table. Three additional versions were made to be store or soda fountain calendars. These were in the smaller 8" x 14" size, and were designed with a vertical inset area wherein the name of an individual soda fountain or business could be imprinted. One version depicts a regulation Coca-Cola glass on the table; another shows a simple, unmarked, straight-sided glass; and the third version depicts a 6-1/2 oz. standard Coke bottle on the table. Why these different variations were produced or considered necessary is not known. Still another version of the full size calendar has surfaced within the last couple of years—one depicting an inset bottle similar to one of the variations seen in the 1927 calendar.

The final Coca-Cola calendar of the decade, issued in 1929, was very similar in look and design to both the 1927 and 1928 calendars. It pictured a brunette model holding a glass of Coca-Cola, with a bottle sitting on a small table to the model's right. The visual theme of most of the 1920s girl calendars was festive, with young women in party dresses. While prohibition should have put a damper on peoples' spirits during this time period, the years which became known as "The Roaring Twenties" saw a country recovering from the sadness and economic hardships of the previous decade which included a World War, several recessions, and a plague in 1918 that cost thousands of American lives. The stock market boomed in the 1920s, and many new millionaires appeared on the scene. Society was in transformation, with many turn-of-the-century inventions, such as automobiles and electricity, becoming commonplace.

Likewise, The Coca-Cola Company had created all-new markets for its soft drink. With the six-pack carrier, Coca-Cola could be consumed anywhere, not just at the soda fountain or corner drug store. Ice coolers were produced, providing gas stations and all kinds of other business enterprises with the ability to sell America's most popular soft drink. However, one thing had not changed since the founding of The Company: Pretty, wholesome models continued to be pictured on calendars, serving trays, and other advertising pieces, and this subject remained a central focus of The Company's marketing efforts.

1920 "GOLFER GIRL"

12" x 32" • type F

"Copyright The Coca-Cola Company" in lower left of print.

PCA044.000

The 1920 calendar was issued in two versions: glass and bottle. There is an interesting scene of golfers in the background of this colorful artwork. With World War I concluded, and Americans finally getting back to their normal pursuits in life, the 1920 calendar was produced in larger numbers than the previous few years. Both glass and bottle versions have turned up in about equal numbers over the years.

1921 "AUTUMN GIRL"

12" x 32" • type F

"Copyright The Coca-Cola Company" in lower left of print.

PCA045.000

There is only one version of the 1921 calendar, displaying both a glass and a bottle. Following the tradition of the previous five calendars, the model represents a wonderful visage of the colorful and beautiful fashion of the day. The artwork also bears an interesting garden scene, complete with couples in the background. The 1921 calendar is considered one of the easiest-to-find of the early 1920s calendars.

1921		JANUARY			1921	
SUNDAY	MONDAY	TUESDAY	WEDNESDAY	THURSDAY	FRIDAY	SATURDAY
						1
2	3	4	5	6	7	8
9	10	11	12	13	14	15
16	17	18	19	20	21	22
23/30	24/31	25	26	27	28	29

1922		JANUARY			1922	
SUNDAY	MONDAY	TUESDAY	WEDNESDAY	THURSDAY	FRIDAY	SATURDAY
1	2	3	4	5	6	7
8	9	10	11	12	13	14
15	16	17	18	19	20	21
22	23	24	25	26	27	28
29	30	31				

1922 "SUMMER GIRL"

12" x 32" • type F
"Copyright The Coca-Cola Company" in lower left of print.
"Forbes, Boston" in lower right of print.
PCA045.000

The 1922 calendar was produced in a single version only, displaying both glass and bottle. Not only is this the most colorful of all the early 1920s calendars, it also boasts the most interesting and detailed background image—a baseball game, complete with grandstand, fans, and players in action. The 1922 calendar is also the last of the longer-type calendars, and it marks the end of the long-standing fashion trend of ladies wearing large and beautiful hats.

1923 "FLAPPER GIRL"

12" x 24" • type F

"Copyrite The Coca-Cola Co." in lower left, under print.

"Made in U.S.A." in lower right, under print.

PCA047.000

The 1923 calendar was produced in two versions: glass and bottle, with both turning up about equally over the years. However, it is interesting to note that the bottle version of this calendar shows a bottle clearly labeled eight ounces—strange because, at the time, there was no eight ounce bottle available, but only a six-and-a-half ounce version. This was also the first of the small "type F" calendars.

1924 SMILING GIRL

12" x 24" • type F

PCA048.000

The combination of both glass and bottle on this artwork eliminated the need for two separate versions. Note the change in the fountain glass from a flared-out lip on the 1923 calendar to the turned-in lip on the 1924 issue.

1925 GIRL AT PARTY

12" x 24" • type F

PCA049.000

The 1925 calendar again incorporated images of both a bottle and a glass, eliminating the need for two separate versions. This calendar art also incorporates interesting background imagery of people at a party. The fox stole and turban-type hat were obviously the fashion of the day. Note the bottle that appears on the ledge next to the model. This bottle does not appear on the corresponding serving tray for 1925. However, it does appear on the 1970s reproduction of the tray, making it easy to distinguish the original from the reproduction.

1926 GIRL WITH TENNIS RACKET

10-1/2" x 18-5/8" • type F

"Copyrite The Coca-Cola Company" on lower left, under print.

"Printed in U.S.A." on lower right, under print

PCA050.000

The size, style, and design of the 1926 calendar was a total departure from previous Coca-Cola calendars. Not only is it a smaller size, but the print portion of the calendar is printed on a lightweight cardstock rather than paper, and the calendar has a simple hole punched at the top rather than a metal strip and hanger. This calendar is also the first to use a cover sheet over the pad. It simply reads "1926," surrounded by an ornate scroll border.

1926

Compliments of The Coca-Cola Company Atlanta, Ga

1927 GIRL WITH BOUQUET OF FLOWERS

12" x 24" • type F
"Lithographed in U.S.A." in lower right,
within the border.
PCA051.000

The 1927 calendar is the first to incorporate an ornate border around the print, with a trademark plate under the image. A bottle version of this calendar displays the bottle in an ornate border at the bottom left side of the print, while another version shows no bottle. Note the distinct fashion change in the model's attire. The Coca-Cola Company also offered a "Dealer" calendar this same year, featuring the same artwork, and it is shown elsewhere in this book.

1928 GIRL WITH FUR STOLE

12" x 24" • type F

"Copyrite The Coca-Cola Co." in lower left border.
"Lithographed in U.S.A." in lower right border.
PCA052.000

The 1928 calendar incorporated both a bottle and
a glass in the artwork, thereby negating the need for
two separate versions. The image on this calendar was
also offered on a smaller "dealer" calendar in a number
of variations. These are shown elsewhere in this book.

1929 GIRL WITH LONG STRING OF PEARLS

12" x 24" • type F • "Copyrite The Coca-Cola Co., Lithographed in U.S.A." in lower right of print.
PCA053.000

The 1929 calendar again used the images of both a glass and a bottle, eliminating the need for two
separate versions. The 1929 calendar is the most difficult to find of all the 1920s calendars.

CALENDAR ART OF THE THIRTIES: DECADE OF THE FAMOUS ARTISTS

The unparalleled marketing sophistication of The Coca-Cola Company was established well before the 1930s, but even in a decade remembered for "The Great Depression," The Company continued its astounding growth. Rather than diminish its marketing efforts, The Company used entirely new concepts in marketing its soft drink. These included the use of many famous movie stars to promote the brand; famous artists to paint the advertising pieces; exposure on national radio programs; and an expanded print media campaign that was employed throughout the United States.

The first Coca-Cola Company calendar of the 1930s featured a girl in a bathing suit, sitting in a canoe. From that standpoint, it was quite an unusual choice for calendar art. While swimsuit girls were commonly used on serving trays and other advertising pieces during the 1930s, this was the only domestic calendar issued in The Company's history that depicted a swimsuit girl. The 1930 calendar primarily focused on the bottle market, in as much as it showed the model holding a bottle in her hand, with another positioned behind her.

That same year, a most unusual calendar was produced for The Coca-Cola Bottling Works of Romney, West Virginia. As in previous years, individual bottlers sometimes purchased advertising materials which were not developed, approved, or distributed by The Coca-Cola Company in Atlanta. In the case of the 1930 calendar made for this bottler, the art differed greatly from that produced by The Company. It depicted a pin-up-art style girl in a provocative pose, with a scene which featured a colorful art deco look. On both sides of the calendar pad, shapely bottles of Whistle soda were included. Obviously, the Romney, West Virginia, Coca-Cola Bottling Works also bottled products other than Coca-Cola, and, as such, wanted to promote multiple brands on their calendar. Since these calendars were purchased by an individual bottler, the number distributed was undoubtedly very small.

The 1931 calendar was one of legendary proportions. Its history will be recounted in this book because it is a history that continues to unfold to this day. One of the favorite of all of the images ever used in Coca-Cola advertising was created by none other than the American Icon artist: Norman Rockwell. By the time Rockwell began working with The Coca-Cola Company, he was already a renowned artist. All in all, he created six paintings for Coca-Cola, all of which were used in various advertising media. Undoubtedly, the most famous Rockwell image of all is the one known as "The Barefoot Boy," which depicts a young, redheaded, freckle-faced boy, accompanied by his dog, in a heart-warming scene which shows him holding a bottle of Coca-Cola and a sandwich. This art was used on a serving tray, cardboard cutout, notepad, blotter, and the 1931 calendar. What is truly amazing is that the model who posed for this memorable picture is still living today, and his story of how he became "The Barefoot Boy" is fascinating. In an interview conducted expressly for this book, he related many new and interesting bits and pieces of information which add insights and color to this chapter in The Company's advertising history.

Chapter 6

This stock calendar, with art by Rolf Armstrong, was used by the Romney, West Virginia, Coca-Cola Bottling Works, which obviously bottled Whistle Orange Soda, as well.

Daniel M. Grant, who is also known as Danny MacGrant, lives in Hollister, California, and he has vivid memories of the events which led to his being selected as the model for the 1931 calendar. His recollection of the time period of the 1930s is a treasure. He is a wonderful gentleman, who willingly shared detailed anecdotes of his memory of meeting Norman Rockwell and becoming "The Barefoot Boy."

Danny MacGrant moved to Southern California from Arizona as a young boy in 1927. His grandfather was taken by his freckles, red hair, smiling face, and arresting personality— so much so that he enrolled Danny in Central Casting, an agency that provided actors and actresses for the motion picture studios. From 1927 until 1933, Danny MacGrant appeared in some thirty-eight motion pictures. One of them was a silent *Our Gang* picture. Others included *Tom Sawyer*, *Huckleberry Fin*, *Sunnyside Up*, *Platinum Blonde*, and *Oliver Twist*, among others. Although he had only a small part in *Platinum Blonde*, Danny has vivid recollections of the stars in that movie, including Jean Harlow and Loretta Young. He remembers Jean Harlow as "stunningly beautiful," and recalls her kissing him on the cheek. He was so taken by the experience that he vowed not to wash his face for days afterwards. Jean Harlow, in addition to being a movie star, was also one of the numerous celebrities who appeared in advertising art for Coca-Cola during the early 1930s.

Danny's selection as the subject for the 1931 calendar, and the circumstances surrounding that event, are well documented. He had been registered with Central Casting for a few years when, in April 1930, he received a call to go to their offices after school for an interview. When Danny arrived, he

Danny MacGrant, in the outfit he wore for the Norman Rockwell painting.

Photo of Danny MacGrant today, posing with the famous 1913 Rockwell calendar that bears his likeness.

was joined by three other red-headed, freckled-faced boys of about the same age. All were asked to line up against the wall, and after they did so, a gentleman with a pipe in his mouth walked in the room to look them over. After studying each boy for a period of time, the man pointed to Danny and invited him (along with his mother) into an office. Once inside, the gentleman introduced himself as Norman Rockwell, and he offered Danny a job to pose for a soft drink advertisement. The fee for his service was to be an astounding $50 per day. At the time, Danny's father made $18 for an entire week's work!

In his own words, Danny described posing for Norman Rockwell:

"I sat and posed for five days, sitting on a straight back chair, with my feet raised on a box. The bottle of unopened Coke, the bread, the straw hat, the denim shirt, and the pants were all furnished. He (Norman Rockwell) was very quiet when he had a brush in his hand, and he was meticulous in getting just the right thing on the canvas. He started by charcoaling the entire picture, going over it many times. He then painted the skin portions, and finished with the clothing, the dog, the open can, and the fishing pole at a later date. When he was painting my foot, he wrapped my toe with a bandage. While he was at the easel, he was very engrossed and quiet, but, during the breaks, he and another gentleman shared many laughs."

It was not until December 1930 that Danny saw the painting, and the finished product. He was invited to a sales convention of Coca-Cola Bottlers at the Ambassador Hotel, in Los Angeles, at which time calendars and trays were presented to the guests. Danny signed many calendars at that event. Subsequently, the local bottler brought hundreds of the calendars to his home, where Danny dutifully signed them for subsequent distribution. Danny retains one of those for his personal collection, along with many other "Barefoot Boy" items.

Over the years, Danny has remained in close contact with The Coca-Cola Company. It is unprecedented to find an individual who had a living part in the development of a famous piece of Coca-Cola advertising nearly seventy years ago, not to mention his memory of one of America's truly great illustrators.

Because Norman Rockwell did the artwork for four Coca-Cola advertising calendars (1931, 1932, 1934, and 1935) it is fitting to note his stature as an American artist. Rockwell was born in 1894, in New York City, and by the time he was eighteen years old, in 1912, he was an accomplished artist commencing his commercial career. At just twenty years old, his work reached an early pinnacle when he was hired to do a cover for the *Saturday Evening Post*, which was America's most popular magazine of the time. Success built upon success when he was selected, in 1916, to do a cover for *LIFE* magazine. His competition for the cover ranked among some of the finest illustrators of the day, including A. B. Frost, N. C. Wyeth, and Maxfield Parrish, among others. His first works for advertisers included Fisk Bicycle Tire, Jell-O, Orange Crush, and Overland

Norman Rockwell's painting of Danny MacGrant was used on other advertising in 1931, including this 19" x 27" cardboard cutout display piece.

Automobiles, to mention but a few. Over the years, his art graced advertisements for products used in all walks of life. He was a giant, who ultimately became America's best-known artist.

From early on, Rockwell's artistic style was that of a visual storyteller. He was a genius at depicting ordinary people in their everyday lives through images that captured the imagination of those who viewed his artwork. Rockwell's work over a lifetime was prodigious, to say the least. Throughout his career, Rockwell painted 318 covers for the *Saturday Evening Post*. His work also was featured on virtually every major magazine, including *St. Nicholas*, *Ramparts*, *LIFE*, *Look*, *Leslie's*, and the *Literary Digest*. His art also extended well beyond magazine covers and commercial products. For years, he was the exclusive artist for Boy Scouts of America calendars, and his work graced murals, posters, and greeting cards. For sixty years, he portrayed and memorialized a unique social history of the United States. The Coca-Cola Company had the resources and foresight to sense the mass appeal of Rockwell's art, and made it an important part of its early to mid-1930s printed advertising program. The Company seized upon the appeal of his art, and urged bottlers to take full advantage of the images purchased to market the soft drink. In the 1931 advertising price list, "The Barefoot Boy" calendar was pictured with the following copy:

"1931 Calendar. Speaks for itself (the picture). Reproduced from a painting by one of America's most famous artists, this calendar is pleasing and full of human interest. Its universal appeal makes it appropriate for any place at all times. Order now and begin your distribution early, so as to derive its full advertising value. The pad has thirteen leaves beginning with December, 1930, allowing you to begin distribution by November 15. The calendars are packed 250 to the case. Place order in multiples of this quantity."

Two million of "The Barefoot Boy" calendars were distributed in 1931, and it is likely that a similar number of serving trays with matching art were issued, as well. Bottlers paid $40.25 per thousand (four cents each) for these calendars, and thirteen-and-a-quarter cents each for the trays.

In 1932, The Coca-Cola Cola Company followed up with another calendar featuring the art of Norman Rockwell. With artwork entitled "The Old Oaken Bucket," the calendar pictures a young barefoot boy with his dog, sitting on the edge of an old well, and drinking a bottle of Coca-Cola. The oak bucket is filled with bottles of Coca-Cola, presumably placed there to keep them cold. The look and appeal of the 1932 calendar is nearly identical to the 1931 Rockwell art calendar, although "The Barefoot Boy" seems to be more highly prized by collectors. Unlike the 1931 calendar, the 1932 art was not featured on the 1932 serving tray, which pictured a girl in a yellow bathing suit.

While the calendar remained a standard of Coca-Cola's point-of-sale advertising effort, The Company continued its relentless march to new growth through other innovative marketing techniques. Beginning in the 1930s, it used the images of movie stars to promote the soft drink in various types of advertising collateral. Many of the most famous actors and actresses of the time were featured, including Jean Harlow, Clark Gable, Johnny Weissmuller, Maureen O'Sullivan, Madge Evans, and many others. Beyond advertising alone, other developments moved The Company forward in its quest for dynamic growth.

During the early to mid-1930s, The Coca-Cola Company used many Hollywood movie stars to promote its famous drink. This cardboard cutout display measures 25-1/2" x 35-1/2", and features Frances Dee and Gene Raymond.

The Chicago World's Fair, in 1933, bore witness to yet another intriguing innovation by The Coca-Cola Company. Visitors to the fair were treated to Coca-Cola dispensed from a machine in which the carbonated water and syrup were mixed automatically. From that point on, the manual mixing of syrup and soda water was a thing of the past. During the same period, refrigerated stand-alone coolers for bottles of Coca-Cola were being designed and perfected. By 1935, the first refrigerated cooler vending machine was offered to retailers. Automation would fuel the engine for further growth by The Coca-Cola Company in the 1930s and beyond.

After using Norman Rockwell art for two years in a row, The Coca-Cola Company chose another illustrator for creation of its 1933 calendar. Frederick Stanley (1892-1967) was another American-born artist who had achieved widespread acclaim for his commercial paintings. His clients included Arrow Shirts, Atlas Tires, Buick, Chevrolet, Keystone Watches, Texaco, Post Bran Flakes, Fuller Paints, and many other national firms. He also created artwork for the covers of numerous national publications, including the *Saturday Evening Post*, *Colliers*, *This Week*, and *Liberty* magazines. During his career, he won several awards for his artwork. Consequently, although far less well-known than Rockwell, Frederick Stanley was nevertheless a fine artist in his own right.

The artwork on the 1933 calendar provides another nostalgic rendition of Americana. It pictures a blacksmith (the artwork is entitled "The Village Blacksmith") sharing a laugh and a bottle of Coca-Cola with a young boy. The cover page features a poem by Henry Wadsworth Longfellow, bearing the same title as the artwork. This calendar is truly another heart-warming piece, recalling a time kept alive by art that tells a story.

For the 1934 calendar, The Company again selected Norman Rockwell as the artist. The picture on the calendar depicts an elderly gentleman and his daughter, seated on a porch in a Southern scene. The lovely young lady is seen holding a fiddle, and she appears to be singing to her father. On the cover page of the pad, the poem "Carry me back to old Virginny," by James Bland, is printed. Recently, The Coca-Cola Company was fortunate to have acquired the original Norman Rockwell painting from which the calendar art was reproduced.

The last Rockwell painting commissioned for promotional use by The Coca-Cola Company was the subject of the 1935 calendar. The art depicted a boy, seated on a log with his dog, fishing pole, and a bottle of Coca-Cola, in another scene that was designed to evoke childhood memories in the viewer. The cover sheet of the pad includes the poem "Out Fishin'," by Edgar Guest. Large quantities of these calendars were produced and distributed throughout the marketplace.

1936 was a very special year for The Coca-Cola Company. This was the year that the firm celebrated its 50th anniversary (1886-1936). Perhaps because it was such a pivotal point in the history of the organization, a famous artist was

Another beautiful Norman Rockwell painting was not only used on the 1935 Coca-Cola calendar, but on this cardboard cutout window display, as well. It measures 18" x 36"; is three-dimensional; and was printed by Snyder and Black.

again selected to produce art for the 1936 and 1937 calendars. This artist was Newell Convers Wyeth. Born in 1882, N. C. Wyeth proved to be a relatively poor student, but at an early age he a showed talent for sketching. In 1902, he enrolled in the prestigious Howard Pyle School of Art, where students were selected for their ability. Wyeth sold his first painting to the *Saturday Evening Post* in 1902. His first works were generally western scenes, reflecting his attraction to the West and his admiration for artist Frederick Remington. By 1911, Wyeth received a commission to illustrate *Treasure Island*—Robert Lewis Stevenson's famous book.

In addition to creating wonderful landscape scenes, Wyeth did a great number of commercial illustrations for use as advertisements. Some of his clients included Quaker Oats Company, General Electric, Joseph Seagram and Sons, Metropolitan Life Insurance Company, and, of course, The Coca-Cola Company, among others. His style was dramatic and bold, as is amply demonstrated in the works he completed for The Coca-Cola Company. Wyeth's rich use of color was exceptional. While he received acclaim during his lifetime, full recognition of his talent occurred only after his death.

The 1936 Coca-Cola calendar is truly a wonderful piece of art. It portrays a young girl talking to a sea captain on a beach, while both are sharing a Coca-Cola. The clouds in the sky over the ocean backdrop are sensational in their detail and rich colors. The copy on the calendar reads "Through all the years since 1886," and the calendar notes that it is the fiftieth anniversary of The Coca-Cola Company. A cover page on the pad bears a wreath with the 50th Anniversary seal on it.

The January 1936 issue of *The Red Barrel* featured the 1936 calendar on the inside cover. On that page is a most interesting letter written by N. C. Wyeth, which tells the story of the painting. It notes:

"When considering a subject for the Coca-Cola calendar, I realized that the picture should symbolize restful coolness, and it was natural and inevitable that I turned to my native New England with its blue and cooling seaboard. To me, the sparkling coast on the North Atlantic typified all that is refreshing and cool. The locale of this picture is a little fishing town not far from the Canadian border. The old salt sitting on the rail of his red dory is a real character whose wisdom and genial sense of humor is a constant delight. I have spent days in his company, fishing, hauling lobster traps, or clamming, and my profit from the association has always been far greater than the mere pleasure of fishing.

Some of his kindly, quality humor I have tried to express in his face and figure—to portray the kind of character and disposition so loved by children such as the little girl shown in the picture with him. Often have I seen him in his red dory, his spirit sail stepped in the forward seat—he holding the sheet, but a delighted little girl or boy handling the tiller. The painting is a page from real life—a page that I loved to paint since the setting and characters are, I feel, a part of my own life."

Thus, in the words of the artist himself, the picture on the calendar presented a real representation of his surroundings. Although not as difficult to locate as many of the earlier Coca-Cola calendars, this one is surely a classic that will increase in value over the years. Beyond that, it has somewhat greater significance than other calendars of its time period due to the 50th anniversary of The Company, as noted on the calendar.

The second calendar to depict the art of N. C. Wyeth is the 1937 issue. This wonderful calendar depicts a boy, with his fishing pole and dog, walking with a mission in mind. It appears that he must be on his way to his favorite "fishin hole." Behind him is a backdrop of a massive cloud formation, with a dramatic interpretation that was clearly Wyeth's trademark style. As with the Norman Rockwell calendar designs, Wyeth calendars are sought after for more than just their desirability as Coca-Cola advertising pieces. The art is so exceptional that they stand on their own merit from an artistic perspective.

In 1938, the Coca-Cola calendar art was the same as that used on the serving tray issue for that year. The illustrator, Bradshaw Crandall, created the art, which showed a pretty young lady holding a bottle of Coca Cola, while seated in front of a closed window shade. Over the years, collectors have referred to this art as the "Girl at Shade." The cover page of the pad stated "Greetings 1938."

The last calendar of the decade of the 1930s featured the typical art-of-choice used on many Coca-Cola calendars. It depicted a young woman pouring a bottle of Coca-Cola into a glass. The cover page of the pad stated "Greetings 1939." While not as alluring an image as many of the other 1930s calendars, the 1939 calendar is nevertheless pleasing in appearance.

In spite of the effects of the Great Depression, the 1930s brought Coca-Cola Company advertising efforts to new heights. Advertising was upscale, with celebrities in vogue, and with new media, such as radio, being widely used to promote Coca-Cola. In 1939, fifty million gallons of Coca-Cola were sold for the first time. Annual advertising expenditures exceeded $7 million. And, in a period of just five years—from 1934 to 1939—74,500 refrigerated Coca-Cola coolers were sold. The automatic fountain dispenser added a new dimension to sales opportunities, as well. The Company had not only weathered the Depression, but had actually thrived during it. Still another decade went by in which the calendar continued to endure as an important part of Coca-Cola's overall advertising and promotional campaign.

Perhaps the most important change brought about during the decade of the 1930s was the establishment of the "take home" market. While this trend began in the 1920s when the first six-pack holder was offered, it exploded in the 1930s. No longer was the soda fountain the primary place where Coca-Cola was served. The soft drink was everywhere—in stores, gas stations, airports, and virtually anywhere else that people assembled. It was in the year 1939 that Frank Sinatra's first hit was heard on coast-to-coast radio. Harry James accompanied his vocal talent as he sang his way into America's hearts with the smash hit "All or Nothing at All." Increasingly, America was advancing in terms of technology and communications, and soon these advances would dramatically impact the way business enterprises marketed their products.

1930 GIRL IN BATHING SUIT, LEANING ON ROCK

12" x 24" • type F
"Copyrite Coca-Cola Co." in lower left border
"Lithographed in U.S.A." in lower right border
PCA054.000

The 1930 calendar presents the first artwork depicting a true "Bathing Beauty." This striking and colorful art also carries the signature of artist Hayden Hayden in the upper right corner of the print. This is also the last calendar to display a standard Coca-Cola fountain glass

1931 "THE BAREFOOT BOY"
(ART BY NORMAN ROCKWELL)
12" x 24" • type F
PCA055.000

This is the first calendar image used by Coca-Cola that did not adhere to the long-standing tradition of "pretty girl" calendar art started back in 1891. The model on this colorful and interesting piece of art by Rockwell is a male: Danny MacGrant. This image of a boy and his dog enjoying a Coke is a classic piece of Americana. This image can also be found on a serving tray, a blotter, and other advertising pieces produced in 1931.

Drink
Coca-Cola
Delicious and Refreshing

			MAY		1931	
1931						1931
Sunday	Monday	Tuesday	Wednesday	Thursday	Friday	Saturday
~ Pause often for refreshment ~					1	2
3	4	5	6	7	8	9
10	11	12	13	14	15	16
17	18	19	20	21	22	23
24/31	25	26	27	28	29	30

1932 "THE OLD OAKEN BUCKET"
(ART BY NORMAN ROCKWELL)

12" x 24" • type F
PCA056.000

Undoubtedly inspired by the popularity of 1931 calendar art, a Norman Rockwell painting was again chosen for the 1932 calendar. This wonderful image of a boy with a bucket of cold Cokes, being watched by his dog, is typical Norman Rockwell. Unlike the previous year, this art was exclusive to the calendar.

1933 "THE VILLAGE BLACKSMITH"
(ART BY FREDRIC STANLEY)

12" x 24" • type F
PCA057.000

The cover page of this calendar features a poem by Henry Wadsworth Longfellow. The image of a blacksmith sharing a Coke with a school boy continues the home-spun rendition of American art started in 1931. It is a classic piece of art.

**1934 "CARRY ME BACK
TO OLD VIRGINNY"
(ART BY NORMAN ROCKWELL)**
12" x 24" • type F
PCA058.000

This Rockwell image features an elderly gentleman and his daughter on a porch, in a southern
scene. The poem on the cover sheet, "Carry Me
Back To Old Virginny," is by James Bland.
Even though original Coca-Cola calendar art
paintings are extremely rare, this magnificent
Norman Rockwell painting is in the archives
of The Coca-Cola Company.

1936 "50TH ANNIVERSARY"
(ART BY N. C. WYETH)
12" x 24" • type F
PCA060.000

Certainly the most colorful of all the 1930s calendars. This fantastic N. C. Weyth image celebrates the 50th Anniversary of The Coca-Cola Company, and includes the slogan "Through All The Years Since 1886," while the cover sheet displays the 50th Anniversary logo.

1935 "OUT FISHIN"
(ART BY NORMAN ROCKWELL)
12" x 24" • type F
PCA059.000

This is the last Rockwell painting used on a custom-designed Coca-Cola calendar. The image of a boy and his dog certainly evoked many a childhood memory. The cover sheet on this calendar features the poem "Out Fishin," by Edgar Guest. The 1935 calendar was presumably distributed in huge quantities, and is one of the more commonly found calendars from the 1930s.

THE "COCA-COLA" CALENDAR FOR 1937

Every American boy is a potential Huckleberry Finn. The spirit of the woods, the fields, and the streams, are his fundamental heritage.

To the youthful fisherman, the magic spell of a meandering and sun-flecked brook, or the mysterious quiet of a shining pond at evening, gives the epitome of adventure and joy.

The spoils of his quest may be but a thin string of a few "sunnies", and a perch and a catfish, but the unconscious spirit of the youthful Isaac Walton comes to life and bequeaths to the grown man an array of memories forever cherished.

The creator of this pictorial tribute to the young fisherman is Mr. N. C. Wyeth, mural painter and well known illustrator of many juvenile classics. His natural and sympathetic interest in children and his ability to catch upon canvas their active life, appearance, and moods are manifested in the above painting.

1937 "FISHIN HOLE"
(ART BY N. C. WYETH)
12" x 24" • type F
PCA061.000

This is the second calendar featuring the art of N. C. Wyeth, and the last in the series of "typical American folks" images started in 1931.

1938 GIRL AT SHADE
(ART BY BRADSHAW CRANDALL)
12" x 24" • type F
PCA062.000

This image of a pretty girl with a wide brim hat, sitting in front of a window shade, brings back the typical "pretty girl" calendar images that have been a trademark of The Coca-Cola Company. A very similar (but not exact) image by Bradshaw Crandall was used on the serving tray for 1938.

1939 GIRL POURING A COKE

12" x 24" • type F

PCA063.000

It's interesting to note that this art depicts a young girl about to pour a Coke into an unmarked tumbler, rather than the traditional fountain glass used on earlier calendars. The cover sheet on this calendar simply reads "Greetings 1939."

DRINK Coca-Cola

Thirst asks nothing more

1939	S E P T E M B E R					1939
Sunday	Monday	Tuesday	Wednesday	Thursday	Friday	Saturday
Have Coca-Cola at home, ice-cold for refreshment					1	2
3	4	5	6	7	8	9
10	11	12	13	14	15	16
17	18	19	20	21	22	23
24	25	26	27	28	29	30

CALENDARS OF THE 1940S

Calendar art of the 1940s displayed images that were intended to keep pace with the changing times and appeal to consumer interests. Hostilities broke out in Europe, and expanded into a Second World War when Pearl Harbor was attacked by Japan in December 1941. Coca-Cola advertisements subsequently displayed patriotic themes, highlighted by pictures of servicemen drinking Coca-Cola. Cardboard signs, calendars, and magazine advertisements exhibited soldiers at work, or returning home on leave to their wives or girlfriends. By then, Coca-Cola was as American an icon as hot dogs and apple pie, and every effort was made in The Company's advertising campaigns to build on that symbolism. One ad featured the slogan "Coca-Cola—the global high-sign," making the point that the man in uniform would be greeted everywhere he went with the drink that stood for happy comradeship. To further build its business, and to show support for the boys overseas, The Company sponsored music programs on the radio, and these were broadcast to over forty-three military bases across the United States.

Coca-Cola calendars did take on a different approach to design in the 1940s. While the first calendar issue in 1940 pictured the typical pretty girl, holding a bottle and glass of Coca-Cola, the 1941 calendar featured a new design that would be used in the years to come.

Rather than displaying a single art design with tear sheets attached for each month of the year, the 1941 calendar had six full-size pages. Each page featured a single art image, with two calendar months featured per page. That meant that six art images were included on each complete calendar. This poses something of a dilemma for collectors! With earlier calendars, framing a calendar meant dealing with only a single image produced for each annual calendar. However, beginning with the 1941 calendar, and extending to all other calendars produced in the 1940s, framing the first page of the full, intact calendar means covering up the art on the subsequent five pages. Adding insult to injury, some of the best art on many of the 1940s calendars is featured on those inside pages!

Cover images on 1940s calendars included, quite naturally, pretty girls depicted in a variety of scenes and poses, always holding bottles of Coca-Cola. The 1941 calendar featured the "Skater Girl" art, which mirrored that used on the serving tray issue for that same year. The 1942 calendar pictured a man and woman with a snowman. The 1943 calendar cover depicted a nurse holding a bottle of Coca-Cola (a patriotic theme, given the significant role of nurses in the war effort). The 1944 calendar pictures a stunningly beautiful woman holding a bottle of Coca-Cola, with the image of the U. S. Capitol behind her. In 1945, the cover scene again depicts a winter scene, with a young woman dressed in wintry clothes.

Perhaps the most popular and collectible calendar of the 1940s features the image of the Sprite Boy, who is depicted on the cover of the 1946 calendar. This art featured a young boy with a symbolic Coca-Cola Bottle Cap on his head. Sprite Boy art was used in many advertisements in the late 1940s, and became a well known image throughout America.

This beautiful oil painting was featured on the cover page of the 1941 calendar. Original artwork used to create the Coca-Cola calendars is extremely rare—almost impossible to find today.

The 1947 calendar features art typical of many of the 1940s calendars, in that it also shows a winter scene. In this case, the calendar pictures a very pretty young girl holding snow skis and poles. As with all of the multi-page calendars in the 1940s, and in decades to come, the pictures and images were seasonal.

The 1948 and 1949 calendar covers depicted pretty girls holding bottles of Coca-Cola. The 1948 image was that of a young lady in a winter coat, pictured from her neck up, while the 1949 calendar displays art of a beautiful woman, seated, and enjoying a bottle of Coca-Cola.

While the calendars described thus far were all issued by The Coca-Cola Company, some individual bottlers also produced advertising calendars of their own. The most notable of these, which included images of Cub Scouts and Boy Scouts, featured the art of Norman Rockwell. These calendars are also very collectible, even though they are not considered as "official" advertising art of The Coca-Cola Company.

Another facet of The Coca-Cola Company's advertising efforts in the 1940s was its production of several foreign calendars. By the 1940s, Coca-Cola was being produced and distributed in countries around the world. This being the case, there was a need to promote the product in foreign languages. This trend continued into the 1950s and beyond, with advertising calendars being produced for many different countries.

The most deadly and tragic war in world history concluded in 1945. Combined with an economy that was still recovering from the Depression of the 1930s, and a world that was changing rapidly, radio and television were quickly modifying the way major companies promoted their products. No longer primarily dependent on printed advertising signs and other point-of-sale pieces to sell products, the importance of advertising calendars, serving trays, and signs was being rapidly diminished.

Until the 1940s, placement of eye-catching printed signs and other point-of-sale pieces throughout the country was the core strategy of The Coca-Cola Company's product-promotion effort. These devices would continue to be used into the second half of the twentieth century, but they played far less important roles than in the past. Massive radio and television advertising budgets ate into printed collateral development. Consequently, while The Coca-Cola Company has produced advertising calendars even into the 1990s, their significance in the overall marketing effort has been greatly lessened.

1940 GIRL IN RED DRESS
12" x 24" • type F
PCA064.000

As with the 1939 calendar, this art shows a young lady holding a Coke, and an unmarked glass rather than a standard fountain glass, indicating that the soda fountain was no longer the primary place where Coca-Cola was served. The year 1940 is also the last year of the "single print" calendar.

1941 SKATING GIRL

14-1/2" x 20" • type G

PCA065.000

The year 1941 marked the first year that The Coca-Cola Company changed the basic design of its calendar. The multi-page, six-print calendar, with two months per page, would continue as the standard for the next forty years.

1942 COUPLE WITH SNOWMAN

14-1/2" x 20" • type G

PCA066.000

The advantage of the multi-print calendars is that it offered collectors six different images. Unfortunately, much of this art is very rarely seen today.

1943 "ARMY NURSE"

13" x 20" • type G

PCA067.000

The first glimpse of the influence of World War II on Coca-Cola's calendars can be seen in the art of this wonderful calendar. The country rallied around the war effort, and the advertising messages of the Coca-Cola Company reflected that support.

1944 GIRLS OF DIFFERENT NATIONS

13" x 22" • type H
PCA068.000

Pretty girls from around the world comprise the theme of this beautiful calendar. Displaying these multi-page calendars creates a real dilemma for collectors. Choosing one of the six images for display is not easy, and separating pages is not an option.

1945 "WINTER GIRL"

13" x 21" • type H
PCA069.000

With the war winding down, the 1945 calendar art again depicts pretty girls enjoying their leisure time. This is a renewed tradition that would continue over the next several years.

1946 "SPRITE BOY"

13" x 20-3/4" • type G
PCA070.000

One of the more popular calendars of the 1940s
is the 1946 version, which features the famous
Coca-Cola icon image of "The Sprite Boy." The
combination of pretty girls and the Sprite Boy
makes this calendar a favorite among collectors.

1947 GIRL WITH SKIS
13" x 22" • type G
PCA071.000

A wonderful collection of "girl next door" art is featured on this wonderful calendar. Any single one of these images would make a beautiful calendar all by itself.

1948 "WINTER GIRL"

13" x 22" • type G
PCA072.000

The evolution in styles and fashion, in a country setting into postwar prosperity, shows on this calendar. The "all-American girl" look that has long been the hallmark of Coca-Cola calendars is successfully continued here.

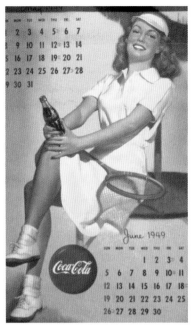

1949 SEATED GIRL
13" x 22" • type G
PCA073.000

The full-figure image of a pretty girl, seated and enjoying a Coke, comprises the feature page of this very attractive calendar. The additional images are equally beautiful, and are rarely seen by collectors.

CALENDARS OF THE 1950S THROUGH THE 1990S

Today, if you were to ask someone off the street to recall advertising of The Coca-Cola Company, they would undoubtedly cite an example of a recent television ad, or, quite possibly, the latest Coca-Cola musical jingle. In the 1920s, that same question would likely have resulted in an individual referring to a sign or a calendar seen in a local soda fountain. Although not as prominent in The Coca-Cola Company's contemporary advertising programs as other more media-oriented promotion, calendars have nevertheless continued to be issued each year. There have also been many foreign calendar issues resulting from the firm's international expansion efforts.

Calendars of the 1950s generally mirrored those of previous years, with attractive young ladies as the central theme of the artwork. In addition to calendars provided to stores and commercial accounts, Coca-Cola also issued a series of calendars that were intended for display in the consumer's home. These calendars were designed to support the advertising message that Coca-Cola "belonged in the home." Most had Santa Claus and Christmas themes on the cover page. These home market "reference calendars" continued to be issued into the 1970s.

In the 1960s, several of the commercial-issue calendars featured young couples in the artwork, and 1970s calendars displayed visual scenes that included flowers and a wide variety of other themes. A group of calendars from 1973-1977 even pictured reproductions of early Coca-Cola advertising art. For example, the 1974 calendar repeated the artwork from the original 1927 calendar. Calendars of the 1980s had various themes of art related to current advertising themes and slogans. Calendars issued after 1960 do not bring significant values in today's collector market, simply because they were issued in such large numbers. Further, most collectors are interested in vintage pre-1960s and earlier calendars. Some of the most interesting post-1950s art is seen on foreign calendars. The 1952 calendar issued for the Mexican market is particularly spectacular. None of this is to say that the future will not bring an all-new group of collectors to the market—a group which finds the calendars of the last half of the twentieth century particularly interesting and desirable.

THE ROLE OF CALENDARS IN COCA-COLA ADVERTISING HISTORY

Calendars have been produced and distributed to promote the Coca-Cola soft drink for more than a hundred years, and they likely will continue to be issued into the twenty-first century. No single advertising medium has been as consistent in The Coca-Cola Company's history as the calendar. A constant theme of all Coca-Cola advertising art is that it is optimistic, wholesome, and youthful. Maybe that is why so many people want to be a part of it by collecting the images depicted on Coca-Cola calendar art. Certainly, no other advertising medium provides the diverse and interesting chronicle of changing times and the evolution of American society as is provided by Coca-Cola's historical advertising calendars.

Chapter 8

1950 GIRL SERVING COKES

13" x 22" • type G
PCA074.000

The first calendar of the 1950s, featuring a pretty girl serving Cokes at a party, is typical of the fun-filled 1950s. Again, the multi-page calendar includes a complete set of beautiful images.

1951 "PARTY GIRL"

13" x 22" • type G
PCA075.000

Entertaining and hospitality were typical themes as a decade of celebration continues with the 1951 calendar. Featuring a girl enjoying a party, this image can also be found on a deck of cards, festoon, and other advertising of the early 1950s. Many of the images used on these multi-page calendars were also used on cardboard signs during the period.

1952 "SQUARE DANCE"

12-1/2" x 22" • type G

PCA076.000

"Coke Adds Zest" is a perfect slogan for this calendar, which features a group of people square dancing. This art was also used on a cardboard sign.

1953 "WORKING GIRL"
12-1/4" x 22" • type G
PCA077.000

Reminding us that Coke is not only for leisure time, but for any time, including work! The slogan "Work Better Refreshed" is a perfect fit.

1954 GIRL AT BASKETBALL GAME
12-1/2" x 22" • type G
PCA078.000

Sports have always played a major role in the lives of most Americans, and this calendar reminds us that being at the game is so much better while enjoying a Coke.

1955 "COKE TIME"

15" x 17" • type G

PCA079.000

Another set of "pretty girl" images adorn this calendar. The beautiful "girl-next-door" enjoying a Coke continues to be the central theme.

1956 "ICE SKATER"
15" x 16-3/4" • type G
PCA080.000

The pin-up art look of this calendar was typical in the mid-1950s. With society changing quickly, teenagers were now becoming a big part of the Coca-Cola market. Calendar art of the time focused on that age group.

The pause that refreshes

January	1957					February						
SUN	MON	TUES	WED	THURS	FRI	SAT	SUN	MON	TUES	WED	THURS	FRI	SAT
	1	2	3	4	5							1	2
6	7	8	9	10	11	12	3	4	5	6	7	8	9
13	14	15	16	17	18	19	10	11	12	13	14	15	16
20	21	22	23	24	25	26	17	18	19	20	21	22	23
27	28	29	30	31			24	25	26	27	28		

"Just what I need"

March	1957					April						
					1	2		1	2	3	4	5	6
3	4	5	6	7	8	9	7	8	9	10	11	12	13
10	11	12	13	14	15	16	14	15	16	17	18	19	20
17	18	19	20	21	22	23	21	22	23	24	25	26	27
24/31	25	26	27	28	29	30	28	29	30				

Good taste

May	1957					June						
			1	2	3	4							1
5	6	7	8	9	10	11	2	3	4	5	6	7	8
12	13	14	15	16	17	18	9	10	11	12	13	14	15
19	20	21	22	23	24	25	16	17	18	19	20	21	22
26	27	28	29	30	31		23/30	24	25	26	27	28	29

Refreshing!

July	1957					August						
	1	2	3	4	5	6					1	2	3
7	8	9	10	11	12	13	4	5	6	7	8	9	10
14	15	16	17	18	19	20	11	12	13	14	15	16	17
21	22	23	24	25	26	27	18	19	20	21	22	23	24
28	29	30	31				25	26	27	28	29	30	31

"I'd love it"

September	1957					October						
1	2	3	4	5	6	7			1	2	3	4	5
8	9	10	11	12	13	14	6	7	8	9	10	11	12
15	16	17	18	19	20	21	13	14	15	16	17	18	19
22	23	24	25	26	27	28	20	21	22	23	24	25	26
29	30						27	28	29	30	31		

For Sparkling Holidays

November	1957					December						
					1	2	1	2	3	4	5	6	7
3	4	5	6	7	8	9	8	9	10	11	12	13	14
10	11	12	13	14	15	16	15	16	17	18	19	20	21
17	18	19	20	21	22	23	22	23	24	25	26	27	28
24	25	26	27	28	29	30	29	30	31				

1957 "GOING SKIING"

12-1/4" x 22" • type G
PCA081.000

The teenage look is obvious on this beautiful piece of art. There is no doubt that calendar art tends to reflect the general mood of the nation. These images provide a perfect supporting example of that notion.

1958 COUPLE WITH SNOWMAN

12-1/4" x 22" • type G

PCA082.000

Not only teenagers, but teenage couples as well, start to emerge as important subject matter for calendars. This art was also used on a deck of cards, as well as in other 1950s advertising.

1959 "BASKETBALL GAME"

12-1/4" x 21-3/4" • type G

PCA083.000

The year 1959 marked an important year in the history of Coca-Cola calendars: the end of the illustrated calendar art era. While artistically created images were used occasionally in the years to follow, the typical and consistent use of painted images came to an end in 1959.

1950S SANTAS

During the 1950s, artist Haddon Sundblom created a series of Santa Claus images for the cover page of each year's Coca-Cola calendar. Because calendars were normally distributed in November of the year preceding the actual year covered by the calendar, this cover page was printed for the month of December of the current year. For example, the full 1952 calendar would have been distributed in November of

1951

1952

1953

1954

1955

1951. The Santa cover sheet, bearing the month of December 1951, would have adorned the 1952 calendar. Sundblom's images are both attractive and nostalgia evoking, and the full assortment constitutes a colorful specialized collection based on a specific theme.

1956

1957

1958

1959

1960

1960 "SKIING COUPLE"

12" x 17" • type G
PCA084.000

The 1960 calendar introduced a new look in Coca-Cola calendars: The first of the "photographic art images" that will be the mainstay of Coca-Cola calendar art from this point on.

1961
12" x 17" • type G
PCA085.000

1962
12" x 17" • type G
PCA086.000

1963
12" x 17" • type G
PCA087.000

1964
12" x 17" • type G
PCA088.000

1965
12" x 17" • type G
PCA089.000

1966
12" x 17" • type G
PCA090.000

1968
13" x 15-1/2" • type G
PCA092.000

1967
12" x 17" • type G
PCA091.000

1969
12" x 17-1/4" • type G
PCA093.000

it's the
real thing

JANUARY

S	M	T	W	T	F	S
				1	2	3
4	5	6	7	8	9	10
11	12	13	14	15	16	17
18	19	20	21	22	23	24
25	26	27	28	29	30	31

FEBRUARY   **1970**

S	M	T	W	T	F	S
1	2	3	4	5	6	7
8	9	10	11	12	13	14
15	16	17	18	19	20	21
22	23	24	25	26	27	28

1970
12-1/4" x 16" • type G
PCA094.000

Durst kennt
keine Jahreszeit

1952

SEPTEMBER								OKTOBER					
Sonntag	Montag	Dienstag	Mittwoch	Donnerstag	Freitag	Samstag	Sonntag	Montag	Dienstag	Mittwoch	Donnerstag	Freitag	Samstag
	1	2	3	4	5	6			1	2	3	4
7	8	9	10	11	12	13	5	6	7	8	9	10	11
14	15	16	17	18	19	20	12	13	14	15	16	17	18
21	22	23	24	25	26	27	19	20	21	22	23	24	25

MISCELLANEOUS & SPECIAL CALENDARS

DISTRIBUTOR CALENDARS

Over the years, many Coca-Cola dealers or distributors who gave away Coca-Cola calendars felt the need to "personalize" the items they were giving to their customers. They wanted their enterprise's name to appear on the calendar. This created something of a problem, since many Coca-Cola calendars have turned up with a sticker or rubber stamp image, bearing the store or distributor's name, placed in a conspicuous place on the print portion of the calendar.

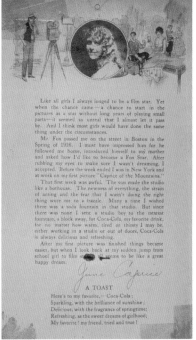

1918 JUNE CAPRICE/DISTRIBUTOR CALENDAR
5" x 9" • type E
PCA041.000

In 1918, The Company offered a small calendar that could be given away by a store or dealer, with space provided at the bottom for an imprinted business name. The reverse side of this calendar explains how June Caprice became a film star, and bears her signature.

1919 MARION DAVIES/ DISTRIBUTOR CALENDAR
6-1/4" x 10-1/2" • type E
PCA042.000

This 1919 distributor calendar did not provide space for a dealer's name to be imprinted.

1916 MIDSUMMER ART/ DISTRIBUTOR CALENDAR

8" x 15" • type C

PCA043.000

In 1916, The Coca-Cola Company produced a small calendar for insertion into a magazine. This calendar featured film star Pearl White, and was called the "Midsummer Art" calendar. It depicted Miss White leaning against a tree, enjoying a Coke.

1927 "DEALERS CALENDAR"

7" x 13" • type E

PCA051.002

This 1927 calendar includes a "privilege panel" at the bottom of the print, providing space for the dealer's imprint. A much more scarce version of this calendar, displaying a bottle, was also produced.

1928 DEALERS CALENDAR

8" x 14" • type E

PCA052.000

This calendar, which also features a "privilege panel," was produced in a number of variations: depicting regulation fountain glasses; displaying unmarked glasses; and a bottle version.

1905 LILLIAN NORDICA "FREE DRINK" AD COUPON

3-3/4" x 7"

PCA053.000

In 1905, The Coca-Cola Company distributed thousands of Free Drink cards, which were attached to an ad featuring opera star Lillian Nordica. These cards were inserted into various magazines. The smaller version of the ad later turned up as small calendars around 1908— the calendar image is actually the top portion of the free drink ad, with a sewn calendar pad stapled to the bottom. This calendar has turned up with pads from the years 1908 through 1911. At one point, collectors believed this calendar to be a fabricated piece from the 1970s, although the fact that it is shown in the April 1949 Coca-Cola Bottler magazine puts such speculation to rest.

BOTTLER CALENDARS

The Coca-Cola Company produced at least one calendar per year starting in 1891. These calendars were initially distributed by The Company and, eventually, by the local bottlers themselves. Nevertheless, many of these bottlers felt it both desireable and necessary to purchase distinctive calendars of their own to be given away to their customers. In most, if not all cases, these individual bottler calendars were stock-issue calendars on which the bottler's name could be later imprinted. These bottler calendars are very interesting and, in most cases, are far more rare than calendars issued by The Company for the same year.

One group of these individual bottler calendars includes a series of stock calendars honoring the Boy Scouts, with artwork by Norman Rockwell. Many different examples of these Boy Scout calendars have turned up over the years.

1915 WESTERN COCA-COLA BOTTLERS

type A

1937

29" x 48" • type F

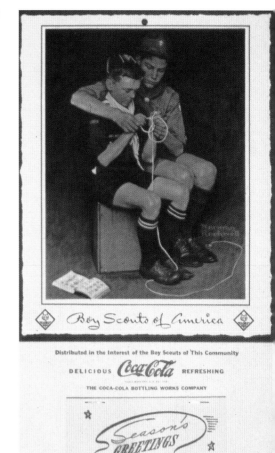

1946 (ROCKWELL/BOY SCOUTS)
6-1/2" x 11-1/2" • type E

1945
29" x 48" • type F • Piqua, Ohio "West Point"

1952
type F • Mason City, Iowa

1949 (ROCKWELL/BOY SCOUTS)
8" x 14-1/2" • type F • Chicago, Illinois

1953 KENTUCKY DERBY
16" x 33-1/2" • type F

1953 (ROCKWELL/BOY SCOUTS)
11" x 23" • type F • Crawfordsville, Indiana

1967

type H • Linton, Indiana

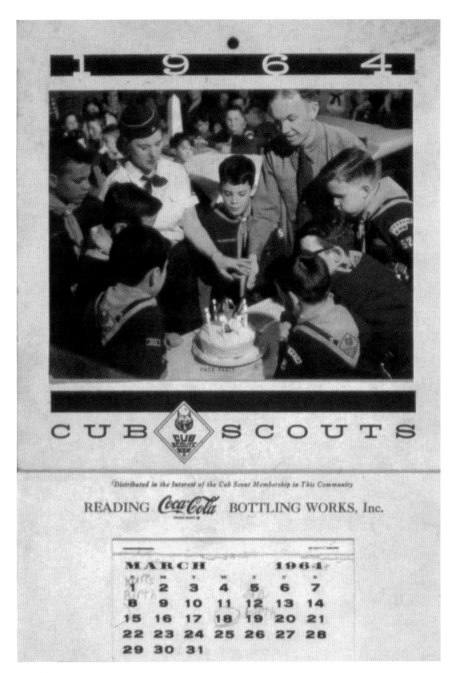

1964 (ROCKWELL/CUB SCOTS)

7-1/4" x 10-1/4" • type E • Reading, Pennsylvania

FOREIGN CALENDARS

Although U.S. collectors have shown minimal interest in Coca-Cola advertising produced for the foreign market, many of these calendars are very interesting and difficult to find. Creative and colorful artwork make these calendars eminently collectible. While the value of these calendars is somewhat less than their U.S. counterparts, they have become more sought after in recent years.

1943 SOUTH AMERICA
14" x 29" • type F

1952 MEXICO

15-3/4" x 27" • type F

1952 GERMANY

type H

1952 GERMANY
type H

1953 BRAZIL

13" x 21-1/4" • type H

1956 EGYPT
type H

1958 MEXICO
11-1/4" x 19" • type H

HOME REFERENCE CALENDARS

From 1954 to 1970, The Coca-Cola Company produced a series of home, or reference, calendars. These are all small-size fold-over paper calendars. Many feature interesting reference

1954 PCA130.000

1955 PCA131.000

1956 PCA132.000

1957 PCA133.000

1958 PCA134.000

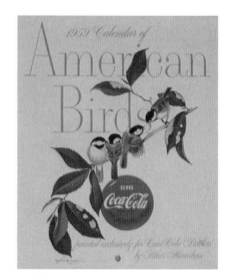

1959 PCA135.000

1960 PCA136.000

1961 PCA137.000

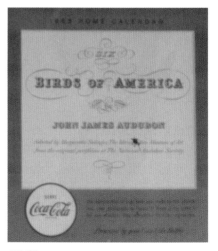

1962 PCA138.000

information, such as birds of America, animals, flowers, and paintings. This group of calendars makes for a great collection, and it is a real challenge for collectors to acquire the complete set.

1963 PCA139.000

1964 PCA140.000

1965 PCA141.000

1966 PCA142.000

1967 PCA143.000

1968 PCA144.000

1969 PCA145.000

1970 PCA146.000

GUIDE FOR COLLECTORS

Few collectibles can compare to an assembled collection of all of the early Coca-Cola calendars when it comes to depicting the way in which American society has evolved over the twentieth century. Unfortunately, today it would be virtually impossible to put together a complete set of calendars dating all the way from 1891 through 1999. There are, however, many avenues which an individual interested in collecting calendars might pursue. Here are just a few suggestions:

• Collect one each of all of the calendars issued during a given decade
  (1920s, 1930s, 1940s, etc.).

• Collect just a few favorite calendars from a certain decade
  (1920, 1922, 1925, 1927).

• Collect a 1920 calendar (for example) and all of the other advertising items that were issued bearing the same artwork, including a pocket mirror, two serving trays, and a change tray.

• Collect a calendar and other advertising pieces issued in one's birth year.

Certainly, the possibilities are endless. As with all antique advertising, CONDITION is paramount to value. For this reason, a mint or very-nearly-mint condition calendar may sell for three times or more what a well-worn or damaged example of the same issue will bring.

Where should you go to buy Coca-Cola memorabilia? Fortunately, historical Coca-Cola advertising is available from many different sources. These include antique shows, shops, the Internet, auctions, and through various antiques publications such as *The Antique Trader*. Some of the greatest finds have even come from yard and garage sales. The Cola Club is a newly founded organization dedicated to the interests of collectors who are interested in vintage advertising (pre-1970). This organization publishes an outstanding newsletter with highly informative articles on all types and brands of historical soda pop advertising.

Grading: Properly ascertaining the condition, or grade, of an antique advertising piece is critical in the process of making an informed purchase decision. Undoubtedly, many readers have heard the expression "it's like new, if you consider how old it is." Always remember that the first calendars looked crisp and wonderful when printed, and were totally new in appearance. Age does not change the parameters of accurate grading. There are rare examples of calendars from the years 1900-1910 that exist, to this day, in as pristine appearance and condition as the nicest 1945 calendar that can be found. Mint is mint! One always wants to make sure that, when buying a calendar promoted at a certain grade, that it is, indeed, properly described and categorized. A grading guide is included in this book. Please take the time to read it carefully. Knowledge rules supreme when buying antique advertising (or any other antique or collectible, for that matter). This book provides the tools needed to help avoid discouraging and costly mistakes.

Trading and Upgrading: Many collectors start collecting with a certain level of quality expectation, and that expectation may subsequently evolve over the years as the collector becomes more astute about the hobby. Usually, as one learns more about a field of collecting, tastes tend to become more discriminating and refined. Calendars offer a wonderful opportunity to improve and upgrade quality over a period of time. As a collection of calendars is acquired, the collector will find that he or she has the option of upgrading. This often involves selling a lesser-quality calendar to help defray the expense of purchasing a significantly better example of the same issue, if and when one becomes available. By following this course, one can gradually, and carefully, develop a very high quality collection.

PRESERVATION AND DISPLAY OF EARLY PAPER CALENDARS

Primary Causes of Paper and Printed Material Deterioration

It is rather amazing that any of the early Coca-Cola calendars have survived the ravages of time. Printed paper is subject to many forms of decay and deterioration, stemming from a variety of sources. It is only through an understanding of the elements that can damage historical papers that an individual can gain some idea of how to properly preserve them. The major causes of damage and deterioration to historical printed papers include:

• Exposure to light: All light sources cause some form of degradation to printed materials, over time. Early calendars and paper signs that were hung in stores and soda fountains were exposed to bright light in window displays and on interior walls. Consequently, most examples of paper advertising materials do show varying degrees of color loss. Red inks, in particular, are most subject to fading over time. Other light sources, such as such as those derived from electrical lighting fixtures, also can damage printed papers. Florescent lighting, in particular, can prove highly destructive to printed papers in a relatively short period of time. On the other hand, calendars and other old printed papers which retain bright and new-appearing colors are those which were protected from extended exposure to ultraviolet degradation and other intense light sources.

• Moisture: Many of the old paper advertising signs located to date have, at some point, been stored in areas where water or high levels of moisture were introduced to the paper surfaces. This results in staining and a heavy accumulation of dust that adheres to the surface of the paper, causing a darkening of the entire piece. Mold may also be present in pieces which have been subjected to excessive moisture.

• Dust and air contaminants: Advertising materials with attractive artwork were often displayed in soda fountains, saloons, stores, and other locations for many years. Yellowing from tobacco smoke and airborne dust can result in a darkening on the paper surfaces, thus diminishing the brightness of both the paper itself, and its printed areas.

• Acidity: Many early advertising signs were printed on papers containing high levels of acid. In time, these acids actually attack the paper and images.

• Temperature and humidity variations: When moisture is driven out of paper, it becomes brittle, and can actually disintegrate over time. All old advertising calendars and posters must be handled with extreme care because they may tear or chip easily due to having lost strength over a period of years.

PROTECTING AND DISPLAYING HISTORICAL PAPER ADVERTISING

The most common way of displaying old calendars is to have them attractively matted and framed. Many vintage advertising pieces have been damaged by framing shops that are not familiar with handling and preserving old printed papers. First, old calendars and paper signs are usually fragile, and they tear easily at the edges. Consequently, extreme caution must be exercised in handling them. If matting materials are used in the framing process, it is essential that they be acid free and of museum preservation quality. The framer must be instructed not to alter the piece in any way (such as removing metal bands). Any use of non-museum-quality tapes to adhere the calendar to the matting materials should also be prohibited. Dry mounting (the process of actually adhering the historical paper to a rigid backing) should only be done at all if it is done by an experienced paper conservationist.

Finally, it is essential that ultraviolet (UV) protective glass be used to protect the framed calendar from light damage. There are protective glass products on the market that are promoted as providing 99% UV protection. Even when UV glass is used, it is important to not display historical calendars and other such pieces in areas subject to intense light sources. Following these simple precautions, historical printed papers will last a very long time, and retain their vibrant colors almost indefinitely.

Some paper preservationists actually use a process to de-acidify old printed advertising materials. Whether a collector chooses to go to this length (and expense) to protect an investment is optional. One way or the other, it is essential that the collector be extremely selective in choosing a source to prepare their valued calendars for display.

RESTORATION

Restoration is a subject which is both controversial and involved, especially when it concerns vintage advertising pieces. Some useful guidelines to consider include:

Best candidates for restoration: Rare advertising pieces that are nearly unobtainable, and which need considerable repairs, may be worthy candidates for restoration. Some of the most common types of damage that can be restored include paper tears, missing paper, staining, and discoloration from darkening over the years. If an item is one of only two or three known to exist, for example, it may actually enhance the value of the piece if it is carefully and properly restored. On the other hand, if a piece is relatively common, restoration may not have a positive impact on the value of the piece.

Inpainting: This is the most difficult process of all! Sometimes an old advertising calendar is found with image areas missing. If it is a rare and desirable piece, it may be necessary to find someone who can recreate the missing image areas to restore the piece to its original appearance. The more of this type of work that needs to be done, the less "original" the piece will be when restored.

Who should restore vintage paper advertising: Perhaps the most important part of the restoration process is finding an individual who is highly experienced and skilled at working with, and restoring, paper. Many a wonderful piece has been ruined by those who thought they could do the work, but who actually had little knowledge of proper restoration practices. Collectors seeking top-quality restorers should call respected dealers and major collectors to determine who is best qualified to do the work. The finest paper conservationists and restorers are usually backlogged with work, and the waiting period for return of a restored piece can be as much as a year or more.

Disclosing restoration work at time of sale: It is essential that the individual owner, prior to the sale of an item, fully disclose details of restoration work done on the piece. If the restoration work is extremely minimal, and the unrestored area of the piece is in otherwise excellent condition, the value of the piece may not be significantly less than what would be assigned to an unrestored piece. Conversely, if there is major restoration, a piece may have value, but it will very likely be far less than that of an original, pristine piece.

GRADING COCA-COLA HISTORICAL CALENDARS

In recent years, vintage and historical advertising signs, trays, calendars, and other materials have increased dramatically in value. This is particularly true of advertising items produced by The Coca-Cola Company over the years. As prices for calendars have increased, providing accurate grading descriptions has become of critical importance to the establishment of fair value. For instance, a nearly perfect 1936 Coca-Cola calendar in pristine condition may well command a marketplace price several times higher than one which is faded, damaged, and stained. Essentially, there are three primary drivers of value or price in the antique advertising market. They are as follows:

Rarity: Calendars produced by The Coca-Cola Company in the first full decade of The Company's history (1890-1900) are exceedingly rare. Regardless of condition, existing examples of these calendars are extremely valuable, and finding a single issue in today's market is nearly impossible. Numerous later issues from the years 1900-1920 are also scarce, and very difficult to locate. Calendars from the years 1920-1940 are more common than those from the early part of the century, but several issues from this time period are not readily available and may require a prolonged search.

Condition: The overall physical condition of an advertising calendar is an important factor in determining its value. Brightness of color, condition of the paper, number of impairments (tears, bends, roll creases), and other visual imperfections are all considerations in assigning a condition grade to a calendar.

Visual appeal: Some Coca-Cola calendars have artwork that is much more compelling and attractive—and, therefore, more sought after—than others in a given period. A classic example is the 1922 calendar, which features a pretty girl with a nostalgic baseball scene behind her. This issue of calendar is no more difficult to locate than other calendars from the early 1920s, but it is more desirable because the graphics are so outstanding, and it has a crossover appeal to baseball memorabilia collectors. As a result, in sales and auctions, this calendar fetches much higher prices than several other issues of the period.

KEY FACTORS IN THE GRADING PROCESS

There are several important criteria which must be considered in grading vintage advertising calendars. Each of these are fundamental to assigning a proper description and numerical grade. They are as follows:

Color: The most common detractor to existing examples of early advertising calendars is faded colors. Calendars exhibiting 20-40% less color brightness than one in mint or pristine original condition are comparatively worth much less. Original calendars with full and vibrant colors, which also are relatively defect-free, are the blue chips of the marketplace, and always will be.

Completeness and originality: Many calendars came with metal bands affixed to the top and bottom of the calendar. Nearly all of them had padded sheets for each month. Calendars which retain original monthly pages and the metal bands are more desirable. Furthermore, missing paper (torn edges, etc.) dramatically reduces the value of a calendar. While original, mint condition calendars with full 12-month pads and pad covers are highly prized, a calendar in wonderful condition, with just one month's tear sheet, may be worth just as much as one with several months worth of pages.

Staining: Many historic calendars were accidentally exposed to water staining. Large stains can darken calendars significantly, and reduce their desirability. Minor staining does not affect value to a great degree.

Creasing: Creases on calendars generally result from the fact that calendars were issued in rolls by the printers, and were often shipped in mailing tubes. Some calendars have minor roll creases, while others exhibit heavy lines that break the paper surface. The degree of creasing, or lack thereof, are important determinants of value and desirability.

GRADING GUIDE

In recent years, the upturn in value of vintage advertising signs and calendars has focused new attention on the process of critical grading. This grading guide will address what we call the "collectible grades." As a result, we will not provide a great deal of detail about grading severely damaged or worn pieces. The major categories of grade or condition are as follows:

Mint Condition: This lofty grade applies only to pieces which have been located in unused and pristine condition. In other words, it must be in a condition equal to the appearance the item exhibited when printed and assembled. There must be no signs of wear, fading, tears, or stains. Calendars in such condition retain a full pad, complete with pad cover. In numerical grading terms, such a piece would rate a full 10 on a scale of 10. In reality, few, if any, totally perfect pieces exist today, although there are calendars in existence which were never used for their intended purpose. Most ultimate grade calendars may have a couple of tiny edge tears, or light roll creasing, or perhaps a minor flaw, and, as a result, grade 9.7-9.9 on a scale of 10.

Near Mint Condition: Calendars in near mint condition are those which were either slightly used or, more likely, unused for their intended purpose. To achieve this grade they must have bright original color, extremely minor flaws, at least one month's pad sheet, minimal staining, and only minor roll creases. Depending on how nearly perfect near mint calendars are, they are graded numerically from 9.0 to 9.9 on a scale of 10.

Excellent Condition: A calendar considered to be in excellent condition may exhibit minor fading, a few small flaws, virtually no missing paper, a minimum of one monthly page, and moderate, but not heavy, roll creasing. Overall, the appearance must be pleasing and very displayable. Such a calendar may also exhibit an edge tear or two, provided that no paper is missing and that the torn area lays flat when matted and framed. Calendars in this category grade from 8.0 to 8-9 on a scale of 10, depending on general condition and the number of flaws.

Very Good Condition: This is the minimal grade for a truly collectible calendar. Such a calendar may exhibit 20-30% fading, but must still retain a relatively sharp and clear image. There may be several notable roll creases, and some minor spotting here and there. Also, it may have some edge tears and/or minor edge mouse chews present, but no major areas of the paper or image can be missing. Calendars in this category grade numerically from 7.0 to 7.9 on a scale of 10. To achieve this grade, the calendar must provide a displayable appearance. Some, or all, of the monthly pages may be missing, as well.

Numerical Grading: Increasingly, numerical grades are being used to describe antique advertising pieces. Their meaning is tied to an educated and knowledgeable estimate of what percent of perfect they are. For example, a virtually perfect caght original color and a full, or partial pad, which exhibits a minor roll crease and a couple of insignificant flaws, may grade 9.0 (or 90% perfect) on a scale of 10. In general terms, numerical grades are variations of condition which relate to general descriptions, as follows:

GRADE DESCRIPTION	NUMERICAL EQUIVALENT
Mint Condition	10
Near Mint Plus	9.5-9.9
Near Mint	9.0-9.4
Excellent to Excellent Plus	8.5-8.9
Excellent Minus	8.0-8.5
Very Good: (collectible and displayable, but showing moderate to considerable visible wear and defects	7.0-7.9

Conditions of less than 7 on a scale of 10 are those pieces which are seriously faded, damaged, stained, or torn. Their future investment potential is definitely limited, with the possible exception of extremely rare early calendars.

Grading is not an exact science, although top dealers and collectors who are highly knowledgeable are capable of rendering very consistent grades. Serious problems may arise with dealers and collectors who misrepresent the condition of items in order to maximize their profits. It is always best to become knowledgeable of market grading, and to only deal with reputable sources known for integrity in their business practices. Consulting with experts before making costly decisions is clearly advisable.

CALENDAR VALUES

ISSUE	GRADE 7.5	GRADE 8.5	GRADE 9.5
1891 Girl w/tennis racket	$9,000	$15,000	$28,000
1891 Girl w/roses	9,000	15,000	28,000
1892 Girl w/butterflies	15,000	25,000	45,000
1896 Lady w/birds	10,000	22,000	35,000
1897 Victorian Girl	8,000	20,000	30,000
1898 Girl w/blue dress	7,500	18,000	25,000
1899 Hilda Clark - 1	6,500	12,000	18,000
1900 Hilda Clark - 2	10,000	16,000	25,000
1901 Hilda Clark - 3	8,000	12,000	20,000
1901 Girl w/pansies	4,500	8,000	12,000
1902 Girl w/feathered hat	6,000	12,000	18,000
1903 Hilda Clark - 4	3,500	7,000	8,500
1904 Lillian Nordica (red)	3,000	5,000	7,500
1905 Lillian Nordica (green)	4,000	6,500	9,000
1906 Juanita	5,500	8,500	15,000
1907 Relieves Fatique	4,500	8,000	12,000
1908 Good To the Last Drop	3,500	7,000	9,500
1909 Exhibition Girl	6,000	9,500	12,000
1910 Happy Days	6,500	12,000	20,000
1910 Hamilton King - 1	4,000	7,500	10,000
1911 Hamilton King - 2	3,500	7,000	10,000
1912 Hamilton King - 3(small)	2,000	6,000	8,500
1913 Hamilton King - 4	1,800	4,500	8,000
1913 Bottlers	5,500	9,000	15,000
1914 Betty	1,000	2,500	4,000
1914 Betty w/bottle	2,500	6,500	9,500
1915 Elaine (glass)	2,000	5,500	9,500

ISSUE	GRADE 7.5	GRADE 8.5	GRADE 9.5
1915 Elaine (bottle)	$3,500	$9,000	$12,000
1916 Girl w/basket (glass)	1,500	3,000	5,500
1916 Girl w/basket (bottle)	1,500	3,000	5,500
1917 Constance (glass)	1,800	3,800	7,000
1917 Constance (bottle)	1,500	3,500	6,500
1918 Two ladies at beach	3,500	6,000	10,000
1919 Girl w/knitting bag (glass or bottle)	2,000	4,500	8,000
1920 Golfer Girl (glass or bottle)	1,300	3,000	5,000
1921 Autumn Girl	800	1,800	2,500
1922 Summer Girl	1,300	2,800	4,000
1923 Flapper Girl (glass or bottle)	500	1,000	1,200
1924 Smiling Girl	700	1,600	1,800
1925 Girl at party	600	1,300	1,500
1926 Girl w/tennis racket	950	1,800	2,000
1927 Girl w/bouquet (bottle)	600	1,300	1,800
1927 Girl w/bouquet (no bottle)	800	1,600	2,000
1928 Girl w/fur stole	600	1,300	1,800
1929 Girl w/string of pearls	750	1,500	2,000
1930 Girl in bathing suit	650	1,300	1,700
1931 The Barefoot Boy	500	1,000	1,800
1932 The Old Oaken Bucket	400	900	1,200
1933 The Village Blacksmith	400	900	1,200
1934 Carry Me Back	400	900	1,200
1935 Out Fishin	300	750	950
1936 50th Anniversary	550	900	1,300

ISSUE	GRADE 7.5	GRADE 8.5	GRADE 9.5
1937 Fishin Hole	$400	$750	$1,000
1938 Girl at shade	500	800	1,200
1939 Girl pouring a Coke	400	700	1,000
1940 Girl in red dress	400	700	1,000
1941 Skating Girl	250	450	600
1942 Couple w/snowman	200	400	500
1943 Army Nurse	300	600	750
1944 Girls of different nations	200	400	600
1945 Winter Girl	200	400	550
1946 Sprite Boy	450	750	1,200
1947 Girl with skis	200	400	550
1948 Winter Girl	185	385	500
1949 Seated Girl	150	300	450
1950 Girl serving Coke	150	300	450
1951 Party Girl	100	200	300
1952 Square Dance	125	200	325
1953 Working Girl	125	200	325
1954 Girl at basketball game	100	185	250
1955 Coke Time	75	125	185
1956 Ice Skater	45	100	125
1957 Going Skiing	75	125	185
1958 Couple w/snowman	65	100	125
1959 Basketball game	65	100	135
1960 Skiing couple	50	85	125
1961	35	75	100
1962	35	75	100

ISSUE	GRADE 7.5	GRADE 8.5	GRADE 9.5
1963	$35	$75	$100
1964	30	65	85
1965	35	70	85
1966	35	70	85
1967	30	65	80
1968	35	70	85
1969	30	65	80
1970	25	60	75
1918 June Caprice	200	450	500
1919 Marion Davies	1,900	4,000	6,500
1916 Pearl White	1,800	3,500	5,500
1927 Distributor	900	1,800	2,800
1928 Distributor	400	850	1,000
1908-1911 small Nordica	600	900	1,100
1915 Western Bottlers	1,800	4,000	5,500
1953 Kentucky Derby	850	1,500	2,200
1952 Mason City, Iowa	450	700	1,000
1937 Coca-Cola Bottling Co.	650	1,000	1,500
1945 Piqua, West Point	800	1,200	1,900
1946 Rockwell Boy Scouts	285	400	500
1949 Rockwell Boy Scouts	285	400	500
1953 Rockwell Boy Scouts	285	400	500
1964 Rockwell Boy Scouts	200	325	400
1967 Linton Ind.	100	150	225
1943-1958 Foreign	Range— $150.00 to $750.00		
1954 - 1970 Home Reference	Range— $8.00 to $40.00		

BIBLIOGRAPHY

BOOKS

Grun, Bernard. *The Timetables of History*. New York. Simon and Schuster/Touchstone, 1991.

Buechner, Thomas H. *Norman Rockwell: Artist and Illustrator*. New York: Harry N. Abrams, 1970.

Hoy, Anne. *Coca-Cola: The First Hundred Years*. Atlanta, Georgia: The Coca-Cola Company, 1986.

Muzio, Jack. *Collectable Tin Advertising Trays*. Santa Rosa, California: Jack Muzio, 1971.

Palazzini, Fioria Steinbach. *Coca-Cola Superstar*. New Zealand: Barrons Educational Series, Inc., in association with David Bateman Ltd. "Golden Heights," 1988.

Petretti, Allan, and Beyer, Chris H. *Classic Coca-Cola Serving Trays*. Norfolk, Virginia: Antique Trader Books, 1998.

Petretti, Allan. *Petretti's Coca-Cola Collectibles Price Guide-10th Edition*. Dubuque, Iowa, 1997.

Strang, Lewis C. *Famous Prima Donnas*. Boston, Massachusetts: L. C. Page & Co., 1900.

PERIODICALS, BROCHURES, AND IMPORTANT DOCUMENTS

Coca-Cola Bottlers Current Advertising Price List. Several of these annual issues for Coca-Cola bottlers were used in the development of this book. These catalogs provide pictures and prices of advertising materials available to bottlers from The Coca-Cola Company.

Garrett, Franklin. *The Black Book/History of Coca-Cola 1886-1940*. Coca-Cola Archives. Franklin Garrett was the Company Historian in the Public Relations Department when this history was compiled in 1940. Unpublished.

Minutes of The Coca-Cola Company. Coca-Cola Company Archives. 1905-1919. Unpublished.

The Coca-Cola Bottler. First published in April 1909, this monthly publication was developed by The Coca-Cola Company for its bottlers. Much information about early merchandising is contained in issues of *The Coca-Cola Bottler*, and this material was used in preparation of this book.

The Red Barrel. First published in January 1926, this monthly publication was issued by The Coca-Cola Company for fountain-service customers. Numerous articles from a variety of these monthly publications were used as important contributions to the book, including pictures.

"The Rise of the American Prima Donna." *Munsey's Magazine*. 1901.

The Chronicle of Coca-Cola since 1886. Published by The Coca-Cola Company.

RESEARCH NOTES:

Information for this reference was derived from a variety of published and unpublished sources. Significant historical data about The Coca-Cola Company was obtained from The Coca-Cola Archives in Atlanta. Additional information about Coca-Cola advertising calendars was derived from the authors' combined 40+ years of experience in collecting, buying, and selling Coca-Cola advertising memorabilia. Both authors have purchased, auctioned, and sold numerous major collections of Coca-Cola advertising memorabilia, including many historical calendars. Allan Petretti is a long-time collector of Coca-Cola advertising calendars, and his personal collection constitutes one of the finest in existence.

Every reasonable effort has been made by the authors to provide accurate information. However, the authors are not responsible for errors or omissions inadvertently made while researching and compiling this work.

ABOUT THE AUTHORS

ALLAN PETRETTI

Having been actively involved in the printing and advertising business, and harboring a keen interest in American history, it's only natural that Allan Petretti would have developed a special passion for collecting the advertising of The Coca-Cola Company. By the early 1970s, he was both a devoted collector and a recognized authority, and he was actively involved with the early groups of organized collectors.

In 1976, Petretti published his first mail-bid auction. Twenty-two years and some 44 auctions later, these semi-annual auctions remain one of the main sources of quality Coca-Cola and other soda-pop memorabilia.

Petretti's Coca-Cola Collectibles Price Guide, now in its 10th edition, is not only considered the "bible" to most collectors, but it has also become the standard by which other price guides are judged. *Petretti's Soda-Pop Collectibles Price Guide*, the most current edition of which was published in 1999, is the only book devoted to the entire soda-pop collectibles field.

Along with co-author Chris Beyer, Allan Petretti also produced the preceding volume in this detailed and definitive history of Coca-Cola collectibles: *Classic Coca-Cola Serving Trays*, published in 1998.

Allan Petretti's many appearances on nationally syndicated television and radio shows include "Personal FX," "Smart Money" with the Dolans, "Watchagot" with Harry Rinker, and "Rinker on Collectibles." In addition, he is a regular talk show guest on radio stations nationwide. Petretti also writes a regular column for the *Antique Trader Weekly* and *Gameroom Magazine*, and he writes frequently for a number of other antiques and collectibles publications. He conducts seminars around the nation for Coca-Cola collector'' groups, and has been interviewed by *The Wall Street Journal*, *USA Today*, *The Robb Report*, and columnists and commentators from around the country. He also conducts appraisals for insurance companies and significant private collections.

Writing about Coca-Cola collectibles, as well as buying and selling them on a full-time basis, Allan Petretti has become one of the nation's foremost authorities on values and market trends relating to Coca-Cola memorabilia.

CHRIS H. BEYER

Chris H. Beyer resides in the Atlanta, Georgia, area with his wife, Gina, and their five children. Beyer and his wife began collecting Coca-Cola serving trays in 1984, and since that time they have become avid collectors of advertising memorabilia in general.

Combining his love of antiques with an interest in the historical development of printed promotional materials, Beyer has written articles for *Collector's Showcase* and *The Inside Collector* magazines. In recent years, he has spent an enormous amount of time and energy researching the historical development of advertising and promotional materials used by The Coca-Cola Company. He was co-author, along with Allan Petretti, of the first volume in this series of books devoted exclusively to vintage Coca-Cola memorabilia: *Classic Coca-Cola Serving Trays*, published in 1998.

Interest in advertising and merchandising comes naturally to Beyer, who serves as the national marketing manager for a major corporation. In that capacity, he does extensive professional writing, and he has authored numerous articles for a variety of national trade publications.

Buy, Sell and Trade With Confidence

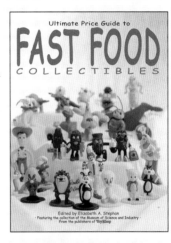
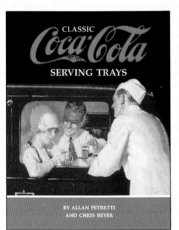

Discover Hidden Treasures In Your Home

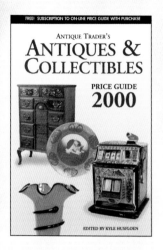
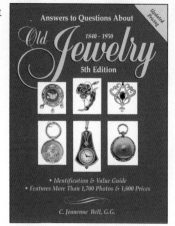
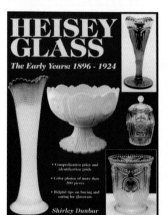

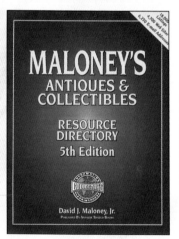
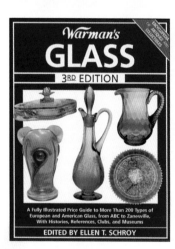

Trust The Experts For Accurate Information

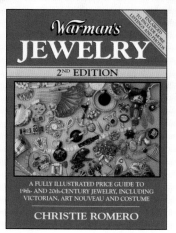

Warman's Jewelry
2nd Edition
by Christie Romero

Offers readers more listings and photos of the most popular and collectible jewelry from the 19th and 20th centuries. It also features the most current prices and gives collectors fascinating and valuable background information in each jewelry category including Victorian, Edwardian and Costume.

Softcover • 8-1/2 x 11
320 pages • 600 b&w photos
WJEW2 • $22.95

20th Century American Ceramics Price Guide
Edited by Susan N. Cox

An enlightening reference guide to collectible pottery and porcelain wares with over 2,000 items in 97 categories produced since the 1920s. Each category begins with a detailed history of the company, and examines recognized names in American ceramics such as Roseville.

Softcover • 6 x 9
256 pages • 500 b&w photos
AT5420 • $14.95

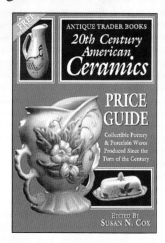

Warman's Depression Glass
A Value & Identification Guide
by Ellen Schroy, Editor

Explore the timeless and very popular Depression Glass collectibles with this up-to-date guide containing descriptions and 9,600 values for nearly 140 patterns. Photos and drawings detail and identify the invaluable patterns such as Adam, Colonial, Jubilee, Old English, Patrick and Windsor.

Softcover • 8-1/2 x 10-7/8
224 pages • 200 illustrations
200 color photos
WDG01 • $24.95

Antique Trader's Pottery & Porcelain Ceramics Price Guide
3rd Edition
Edited by Kyle Husfloen

Drawing on the expertise of Antique Trader Weekly, this volume covers the full range of ceramic products produced in the U.S., England and Europe from the 18th century through the mid-20th century. A convenient format, comprehensive listings and numerous photographs make it easy to locate and identify individual makers and their items. This volume also provides historical information and a variety of useful collecting tips.

Softcover • 6 x 9 • 416 pages
500 b&w photos • 50 color photos
PPOR3 • $18.95

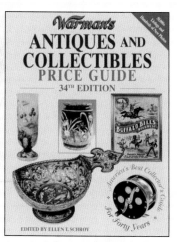

Warman's Antiques and Collectibles Price Guide
34th Edition
Edited by Ellen T. Schroy

This all-new edition offers more than 500 categories, 50,000 updated price listings and hundreds of photos. Major categories covered include advertising, Coca-Cola items, Depression glass, dolls, glassware, politics, sports and toys. This year's edition features a new category of American Paintings, more-detailed furniture and silver listings, and record-breaking prices.

Softcover • 8-1/4 x 10-7/8
640 pages • 600 b&w photos
WAC34 • $17.95

American & European Decorative & Art Glass Price Guide
Edited by Kyle Husfloen

Exquisite and rare decorative glassware from the United States and around the world are highlighted in this abundantly illustrated price guide. Features Amberina, Satin, Burmese, Webb, and Venini with detailed descriptions, accurate prices, and sketches of company marks. Features a special feature on art glass by Bob Rau.

Softcover • 6 x 9
208 pages • 300 b&w photos
AT5498 • $15.95

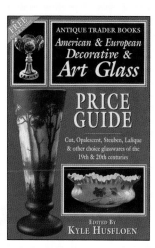

For a FREE catalog or to place a credit card order
Call **800-258-0929** Dept. ACBR
M-F, 7 am - 8 pm • Sat, 8 am - 2 pm, CST

Shipping and Handling: $3.25 1st book; $2 ea. add'l. Call for UPS rates. Foreign orders $15 per shipment plus $5.95 per book.

Sales tax: CA 7.25%, IA 6%, IL 6.25%, PA 6%, TN 8.25%, VA 4.5%, WA 8.2%, WI 5.5%

Satisfaction Guarantee: If for any reason you are not completely satisfied with your purchase, simply return it within 14 days and receive a full refund, less shipping.

krause publications
700 East State Street • Iola, WI 54990-0001
715/445-2214 • FAX: 715/445-4087 • www.krause.com

BOOKS AMERICANA

Warman's

Wallace Homestead

ATB